# *Pilgrims*
## TO THE
# MANGER

Text copyright © Naomi Starkey 2010
The author asserts the moral right
to be identified as the author of this work

**Published by**
**The Bible Reading Fellowship**
15 The Chambers, Vineyard
Abingdon OX14 3FE
United Kingdom
Tel: +44 (0)1865 319700
Email: enquiries@brf.org.uk
Website: www.brf.org.uk
BRF is a Registered Charity

ISBN 978 1 84101 709 9

First published 2010
Reprinted 2010
10 9 8 7 6 5 4 3 2 1
All rights reserved

**Acknowledgments**
Unless otherwise stated, scripture quotations are taken from the Holy Bible, Today's New
International Version, copyright © 2004 by International Bible Society, and are used by
permission of Hodder & Stoughton Publishers, a member of the Hachette Live UK Group. All
rights reserved. 'TNIV' is a registered trademark of International Bible Society.

Extracts from the Authorised Version of the Bible (The King James Bible), the rights in which
are vested in the Crown, are reproduced by permission of the Crown's Patenetee, Cambridge
University Press.

Extracts from The Book of Common Prayer of 1662, the rights of which are vested in the
Crown in perpetuity within the United Kingdom, are reproduced by permission of Cambridge
University Press, Her Majesty's Printers.

'Wrong' by R.S. Thomas, taken from R.S. Thomas, *Collected Later Poems 1988–2000* (Bloodaxe
Books, 2004). Used by permission.

A catalogue record for this book is available from the British Library

Printed in Great Britain by CPI Bookmarque, Croydon

# *Pilgrims*
## TO THE
# MANGER

*Exploring the wonder of God with us*

NAOMI STARKEY

*This book is dedicated to Mike, with very much love, for sharing more than 25 years of thinking, talking and listening.*

## Acknowledgments

*Thanks to Rachel Boulding, Gilly Charkham, Andrew Jones and Mike Starkey for reading the draft text and offering insightful thoughts and encouraging words. Thanks, too, to Sharon for childcare beyond the call of routine auntie duty, so that I had space to start this book.*

# CONTENTS

# WRONG?

*Where is that place apart*
*you summon us to? Noisily*
*we seek it and have no time*
*to stay. Stars are distant;*
*is it more distant still,*
*out in the dark in the shadow*
*of thought itself? No wonder*
*it recedes as we calculate*
*its proximity in light years.*

*Maybe we were mistaken*
*at the beginning or took later*
*a wrong turning. In curved space*
*one can travel for ever and not recognise*
*one's arrivals. I feel rather*
*you are at our shoulder, whispering*
*of the still pool we could sit down*
*by; of the tree of quietness*
*that is at hand; cautioning us*
*to prepare not for the breathless journeys*
*into confusion, but for the stepping*
*aside, through the invisible*
*veil that is about us into a state*
*not place of innocence and delight.*
R.S. THOMAS [1]

*

# INTRODUCTION

'Christmas isn't what it used to be!' I was twelve years old, sitting on my bed, tears trickling down my cheeks as I gazed out in a melodramatic verge-of-adolescence way at the rooftops of suburban Cambridge. My mother hovered in the doorway, trying to make sense of my mood amid the 1001 tasks of a family Christmas Eve.

While I had known for years that there was no Father Christmas (although I pretended, to keep my younger siblings happy), what triggered my despair was finding that I no longer felt the magic. *I wasn't excited any more.* I knew the stories of baby Jesus inside out and back to front; I was still up and about when my mother was filling the stockings; I knew that Christmas dinner was followed by mountains of washing up. I would go to bed on 24 December, wake up next morning and, yes, there would be presents—but in the end it was just another day, followed by the next, and the next.

Thankfully, life has moved on in all kinds of ways since then. I have come to realise the difference between knowing Bible stories and understanding their message; I have learned the pleasures of giving as well as receiving; I have discovered the blessed invention that is the dishwasher. When my own daughter was born at the end of November one year, she appeared as the Christmas morning sermon illustration—and I found that all the carols about mother and baby acquired special resonance.

Christmases continue to come and go, though, and each

year the turn of the seasons seems to happen faster. The round-robin letters, which I for one always enjoy, start to change. Instead of announcing the latest baby, music exam grade or Brownie badge, the news is of children starting to scatter from the family home to further education, jobs or travel. For my parents' generation, there is the shock of familiar names beginning to disappear from the Christmas card list, couples of names dwindling to one on its own. The letters are increasingly dominated by health issues and the upheavals of retirement and downsizing.

It may be, too, that as we try to sum up our news for family and friends, we face the uncomfortable truth that life hasn't turned out quite as we expected. Somehow or other, we never did get that promotion. Yes, our marriage held together but we keep thinking about that old flame we met at the school reunion. Thanks to the economic climate, our dreams of trading up to a more commodious house have evaporated, at least for now. Then there's our relationship with God. Yes, we go to a lovely church but somehow the worship doesn't touch us in the same way any more. Same old hymns, same old Bible readings, same old sermons that leave us feeling vaguely—or sometimes specifically—guilty. And, dare we say it to ourselves, 'Same old God'?

This book of readings is an invitation to pilgrimage, to accompany me through the weeks of Advent, to Christmas itself and on to Epiphany. As the days and weeks pass, we will reflect together on a range of issues—the significance of the festivities, the deeper values that underpin our lives, some of the other special days in the Church calendar at this season, and how we can begin to deepen our understanding of God's perspective on our world, our church and ourselves.

'Pilgrimage' is more than a figure of speech in this book,

however. I invite you to join an imaginary group of pilgrims whose path takes them from a city centre high street, out to the suburbs, beyond the city to a mountain top (don't worry—it's not very high), and then back into the city to find the cathedral, where we rest for the celebrations surrounding Christmas Day itself. In the following days, we travel beyond the streets and down to the sea, where this book concludes. It's not a conventional pilgrimage. It does not follow a well-trodden route to a well-known destination, although we will pass familiar landmarks; it is a pilgrimage of both head and heart in that our aim is to learn more of God and allow ourselves to be challenged by what we discover as we journey together. Above all, we will discover the truth of Immanuel: God is here, everywhere, present with us, if only we will look up and notice him walking alongside us.

# Eat, drink and be merry

Our pilgrimage begins in a familiar place: the shopping mall, the modern temple of our towns and cities. This is not an endearingly tatty little concrete precinct but a gleaming air-conditioned world-within-a-world, hosting the choicest of retail chains. As we walk the levels and ride the escalators, our eyes are dazzled by the tinsel hangings, our ears soothed by seasonal background music. Looking at the faces in the crowds pursuing the UK's number one leisure activity (shopping, in case you weren't sure), we see many that are grimly focused, some (fewer, admittedly, unless you count the teenage girls) relaxed and smiling. Some clutch long lists, others consult mobile phones as they hunt for celebratory clothes, gifts for all manner of loved ones, enough food for days of feasting.

As we stroll through the crowds, what we might find echoing through our minds are the platitudes of a typical off-the-peg Christmas sermon or school assembly—because the idea of eating, drinking and merrymaking is so frivolous, isn't it? And life is so materialistic these days, not like olden times when boys and girls used to look forward to finding a lump of coal and sixpence in their well-darned stocking, and, if they were really, really lucky, an orange. Look at those hordes of parents staggering along with multiple plastic shopping bags from multiple toyshops. Chances are that their children would be just as happy playing with a cardboard box. And are those young men throwing a party or are they going to drink all that wine themselves?

The trouble with the denunciations of the typical off-the-peg Christmas sermon is that they start to look a little shaky as we begin to delve into scripture, and especially when we take a closer look at the life and teaching of the grown-up Jesus. We find that the reign of God is more often associated with generosity, lavishness and celebration than with abstinence and self-denial. Might it be possible that, rather than standing outside the mall and handing out leaflets denouncing consumerism, Jesus might just be stocking up on nuts and drinks, ready to have his friends round—and that we're invited?

*

## 1 December

# PRESENTS

Six days before the Passover, Jesus came to Bethany, where Lazarus lived, whom Jesus had raised from the dead. Here a dinner was given in Jesus' honour. Martha served, while Lazarus was among those reclining at the table with him. Then Mary took about half a litre of pure nard, an expensive perfume; she poured it on Jesus' feet and wiped his feet with her hair. And the house was filled with the fragrance of the perfume. But one of his disciples, Judas Iscariot, who was later to betray him, objected, 'Why wasn't this perfume sold and the money given to the poor? It was worth a year's wages.' ... 'Leave her alone,' Jesus replied. 'It was intended that she should save this perfume for the day of my burial. You will always have the poor among you, but you will not always have me.'
JOHN 12:1–8 (ABRIDGED)

As our shopping mall visit reminds us (as if we needed reminding), the linchpin of Christmas for the vast majority of people is the buying and giving of presents. For some, the shopping comes in a frenzy in the last week before The Day, while most of us will know somebody who starts squirrelling away gifts for the following year, bought in the New Year sales. A more recent phenomenon is that of people going online after their Christmas dinner to sell unwanted presents on eBay.

Every Sunday colour supplement and consumer magazine runs features suggesting the perfect gift for the man/woman/

boy/girl/dog in your life, nuanced as to whether they are sporty or arty, bookish or outdoor (no doubt somebody somewhere includes the dog in such reckoning). In a relatively cash-rich, time-poor economy, the idea of making our own presents tends to remain at the level of guilt-inducing fantasy. We may dream of fashioning our friends pen pots from empty tins covered with shiny foil or presenting family members with handcrafted boxes of home-made fudge—and decide with relief that they would be happier with a scented candle or plain hard cash.

Our attitude to Christmas presents can be ambivalent. While we know that the correct response to the issue is that 'it is more blessed to give than to receive' (Acts 20:35), most of us, while not wanting to appear greedy or materialistic, will admit that we enjoy getting presents ourselves. When it comes to deciding what to give to whom, we may have to strive to reach a working consensus with our consciences: we don't want to be spendthrift but neither do we want to appear miserly. How about settling this year for gifts for close family and friends only, sticking to a limited budget, and being needs-driven rather than wants-driven? Then along comes this passage from John's Gospel, with its shocking display of generosity.

The same story is told, with variations of detail, in all four Gospels (see Matthew 26:6–13; Mark 14:3–9; Luke 7:36–50). It is in John's Gospel that the woman is identified as Mary, sister of Martha and Lazarus, and the critical disciple as Judas Iscariot. No reason is given for Mary's action; the inference is that it was an expression of love, honour and worship for her friend and Lord. She gave to him—not politely offering a token, tasteful gift but bestowing an anointing that was extravagant, reckless and indecorous.

Mary didn't simply offer Jesus a bottle of bog-standard cologne for refreshment. Pure nard was one of the most expensive and aromatic perfumes in the ancient world; as Judas pointed out, the gift was worth a year's wages. We could perhaps reckon an equivalent value of around £11,500, assuming the minimum wage. In a culture where women waited on the men while they ate and talked (a pattern still familiar in many parts of the world today), this woman grovelled at Jesus' feet. How else could she have wiped his feet with her hair, which she shockingly unloosed in public? And feet were considered unclean: again, today it is still considered the height of bad manners in some countries to point your feet at somebody.

Judas' plea to remember the poor surely strikes us as an appropriate response. Jesus could have stopped Mary when she had used, say, a quarter of the precious perfume. But he didn't draw back, politely but firmly telling her to pull herself together, that that was really quite enough. Shouldn't a good rabbi have seized every opportunity to impress his teaching on his followers? While Jesus did respond to Judas' criticism, he also seemed to enjoy the whole anointing experience. Perhaps this incident was the final straw for Judas. Maybe this was the moment when he decided that Jesus was too subversive, too far outside his comfort zone to merit continued loyalty.

Now, we should always bear in mind that the Bible is not a car repair manual. It is not a matter of reading a section and then going off to follow it to the letter. We need to read with an awareness of context, of the original intention of the text and any issues of interpretation, bearing in mind the values of the whole of scripture. This passage is not a divine decree that we should spend £10,000 on a five-star spa package for our church leader, somewhere hot and exotic—although that's not to say we shouldn't, either! There are many places in the Bible where we are told to care for the poor, and places where we are told of the importance of careful stewardship, but here we are also told that our God loves generosity. In Mary's act of love and worship, it was both the gift and the thought that counted. In receiving and honouring her gift, no matter how culturally and morally tasteless it might have seemed to the onlookers, Jesus affirmed both giving and receiving. He warmly affirmed that which was given from the impulse of a loving heart.

As we ponder our own gift-giving, it is worth spending a bit of time thinking about why we are giving, instead of focusing only on what we give. If we are honest, we may have to acknowledge that we are, in fact, trying to buy affection and affirmation; we give because we want the 'thank you' letter rather than because we are freely offering a token of our love to others. On the other hand, perhaps we give out of guilt, knowing that while we haven't been particularly mindful of our loved ones, at least we're filling their stockings or pillow cases with the best that we can afford. Again, we should admit to ourselves that this is not really giving; this is purchase.

Why do we give gifts at Christmas? Although it's the opening line of a standard Christmas morning children's talk, the standard answer bears repeating. Whatever other traditions we may be consciously or unconsciously echoing, we give Christmas presents as a reminder of God's gift—his present to us of his own Son, a reckless offering, generosity beyond reason. What do we think about this gift of God? It may have been some time since we mentally stopped in our tracks and turned our hearts to reflecting on whom God has given and why, and what our response should be. We may find that we are ready to receive—or perhaps we are forced to admit that such lavishness actually fills us with a sense of unworthiness, almost embarrassment. We know that we should give of ourselves—our time, our money, our abilities—to God, but somehow we find it much harder to fathom that God should want to give of himself to us.

## A prayer

*Father God, open our eyes to see you as we journey through this Advent season; open our hearts to the immensity of your love; open our hands to receive all that you promise us in your Son. Amen*

\*

## 2 December

# EATING

Jesus spoke to them again in parables, saying: 'The kingdom of heaven is like a king who prepared a wedding banquet for his son. He sent his servants to those who had been invited to the banquet to tell them to come, but they refused to come. Then he sent some more servants and said, "Tell those who have been invited that I have prepared my dinner: my oxen and fattened cattle have been slaughtered, and everything is ready. Come to the wedding banquet." But they paid no attention and went off… Then [the king] said to his servants, "The wedding banquet is ready, but those I invited did not deserve to come. Go to the street corners and invite to the banquet anyone you find." So the servants went out into the streets and gathered all the people they could find, the bad as well as the good, and the wedding hall was filled with guests.'
MATTHEW 22:1–10 (ABRIDGED)

On this second day of our Advent pilgrimage, it is time to exit the shopping mall and make our way to the market square, where we are lucky enough to discover an abundance of food stalls and traders, threatened but not yet wiped out by the vast supermarkets that have settled further out of town.

Along with presents, food is the other foundational aspect of the season. The association of Christmas with mouth-watering abundance is memorably captured by Charles Dickens, as Scrooge meets the Ghost of Christmas Present:

*Heaped up upon the floor, to form a kind of throne, were turkeys, geese, game, poultry, brawn, great joints of meat, sucking-pigs, long wreaths of sausages, mince-pies, plum-puddings, barrels of oysters, red-hot chestnuts, cherry-cheeked apples, juicy oranges, luscious pears, immense twelfth-cakes, and seething bowls of punch.*[2]

Time to stop reading and go and get a snack...

The dinner is, of course, the centrepiece of the Day itself, a dauntingly complex, quasi-military operation that tests the courage of any would-be domestic god or goddess. We may be adherents of Jamie or Delia; we may swear by turkey or goose; we may incorporate particular family food traditions (fish on Christmas Eve, Buck's Fizz for Christmas breakfast)— but the significance of that central feast remains preeminent, even if it means that hardened traditionalists in the southern hemisphere end up forcing down a roast dinner in sweltering summer heat.

Generally the reason given for the importance of the Christmas feast is that this is a folk memory of pagan festivities. We eat turkey or goose, pudding, mince pies and handfuls of honey-roasted nuts because, in the remote past, our ancestors warded off the effects of the bone-chilling midwinter by scoffing roast ox and swigging mead in a smoky hall. Like other pre-Christian customs, the feast was absorbed into the Church's celebration of Christmas. Furthermore, it represented a breaking of the Advent fast, the discipline that prepared both body and soul for twelve days of rejoicing.

Sadly, the fasting, rather than the feasting, has proved a handy stereotype for what too many perceive as the life-denying, energy-sapping nature of the Church. The Danish film *Babette's Feast* (1987) and the bestselling novel *Chocolat* (Joanne Harris, 1999, also later filmed) both contrast an oppressive, grimly puritanical religiosity with celebratory, sensuous normality, where people are not afraid to enjoy themselves with the good things of this world. It's interesting, not to say bizarre, then, that when Jesus is thinking of another analogy for the kingdom of heaven, he comes up with a wedding feast. And this was not a drinks-and-nibbles affair but a real blow-out with presumably sufficient 'oxen and fattened cattle' to satisfy even the hungriest Anglo-Saxon raider.

As we saw yesterday, it is important to read the Bible sensibly. Jesus is not saying that conspicuous overconsumption of party food is an essential part of following him. What he is saying is that there is something in the lavish scale and over-abundance of such celebrations that speaks to us of the nature of our God. In a society based on subsistence farming, debilitating hunger—even starvation—was no more than one bad harvest away. An invitation to an all-you-can-eat-and-more wedding banquet was an enormous privilege, and yet in the parable the offer is scorned. The king wants his guests to eat until they are stuffed to the eyebrows, but they turn him down.

This parable speaks to us of God's open-handed generosity, as Jesus' response to Mary's gift did in our reading yesterday, but this time we are asked to reflect on more than the personal relationship between giver and recipient. This is a call to table fellowship as the family of God, to sit down in the company of our brothers and sisters and enjoy the feast. A look at the context of this story in Matthew's Gospel suggests that the 'them' of our opening verse implies not only 'the crowd' (21:46) but also 'the chief priests and the Pharisees' (v. 45). Jesus was speaking to the religious authorities and asking whether they were willing to accept what God was offering. Their response is revealed in 22:15: 'Then the Pharisees went out and laid plans to trap him in his words'.

What about us—do we accept God's offer? Do we want to take our seats, dress appropriately (the final lines of the parable sound a cautionary note, vv. 11–14), and join in the fun? We should bear in mind that the parable tells of a feast that will go ahead even though the originally invited guests do not bother to attend. The kingdom of God is among us, whether we like it or not, whether we care or not. If we decline the invitation, we will not be forced to be unwilling guests, for what host makes attendance compulsory except some kind of tyrant? If we postpone our acceptance for too long, though, we may just find that we have left it so late that the doors have shut.

Meanwhile, as we finalise the plans for our own Christmas feasts, we confront a very practical issue, unimaginable to the original audience of Jesus' parable. Today those of us in the developed world live not in a subsistence economy but one in which we have to learn to cope with excess. Our genes are programmed to store fat for times of lean, but when food is plentiful and cheap, even though not necessarily nourishing, we could, if we so chose, literally eat ourselves to death. Our reading affirms that God welcomes us to feast with him; as we prepare today to celebrate his birth with our family and friends, we face the challenge of making sure we know what 'enough' means. It is tragic that modern 'body image' agendas have driven many women and increasing numbers of men to view food as something with which to punish their bodies, either by denying it to themselves or, in effect, using it for a kind of substance abuse.

This is an issue that merits a book in itself, but here we

can simply pause and ask ourselves: why are we eating? Are we really feasting to celebrate—or to fill an emotional gap within? For some, food becomes unhelpfully equated with love, and clearing a plate with 'being good' and the reward of dessert, whether or not we are still hungry. Food is a blessing; let us thank God for it but always remember to keep it in its true place, neither abusing it nor fearing that we cannot control it.

## For reflection

*'Go, eat your food with gladness, and drink your wine with a joyful heart, for God has already approved what you do'* (Ecclesiastes 9:7).

✶

*3 December*

# DRINKING

A wedding took place at Cana in Galilee. Jesus' mother was there, and Jesus and his disciples had also been invited to the wedding. When the wine was gone, Jesus' mother said to him, 'They have no more wine.' 'Woman, why do you involve me?' Jesus replied. 'My hour has not yet come.' His mother said to the servants, 'Do whatever he tells you.' Nearby stood six stone water jars, the kind used by the Jews for ceremonial washing, each holding from eighty to a hundred and twenty litres. Jesus said to the servants, 'Fill the jars with water'; so they filled them to the brim. Then he told them, 'Now draw some out and take it to the master of the banquet.' They did so, and the master of the banquet tasted the water that had been turned into wine... Then he called the bridegroom aside and said, 'Everyone brings out the choice wine first and then the cheaper wine after the guests have had too much to drink; but you have saved the best till now.'

JOHN 2:1–10 (ABRIDGED)

Leaving the market square (perhaps with a small bag of something nice to keep us going), we walk along the high street, passing a selection of pubs and bars ranging from the salubrious to the distinctly dodgy, as well as a couple of busy off-licences. For a significant majority of people, drinking, especially at Christmas, means alcohol, and drinking alcohol all too often means drinking to excess. While adherents of a number of religions, including Christianity, would disapprove of such behaviour, or even actively condemn it, their attitudes are generally seen as eccentric at best.

Forget about learning to appreciate fine wine or savouring a well-aged single malt: despite governmental efforts to introduce a 'Mediterranean-style drinking culture' to the UK, far too many town and city centres become binge drinking zones at weekends. Heavy drinking—and the resultant loss of control—is a fearsome rite of passage that teenagers have to negotiate their way through or bypass. Even if they resolutely choose abstinence, they still have to find a way of carrying on a decent social life in a culture characterised by over-consumption of alcohol.

It was probably to do with growing up in a vicarage, where the door was open to all manner of callers, but I can think of more than a few people I have known personally who were damaged by long-term alcohol abuse. Even if they had a powerful experience of God's love, they often continued to struggle with their addiction. There was no easy healing for the godfather of a close friend of mine. He had an infectious smile and a passion to share his faith, yet he battled unsuccessfully for years with alcoholism and was eventually found lying dead in a park one day.

Like the other seasonal delights that we have considered so far this week, alcohol is yet another that can be a source of perfectly legal pleasure but can so easily be abused, with catastrophic consequences. It can be another means of anaesthesia, a way of drowning a sense of social inadequacy, an apparently easy short cut to being the life and soul of the party.

The Bible has a fair bit to say about drunkenness. In Proverbs 23:31–32, for example, we read, 'Do not gaze at wine when it is red, when it sparkles in the cup… In the end it bites like a snake and poisons like a viper'. We read that wine gladdens the heart (see Psalm 104:15) but we also find stories such as the further adventures of Noah (the bit that doesn't make it into children's Story Bibles), where he plants a vineyard and samples the vintage so enthusiastically that he ends up lying naked and shamed in his tent, in full view of the extended family (Genesis 9:20–27).

Our Bible passage shows Jesus at a wedding party, where he performs 'the first of the signs through which he revealed his glory' (v. 11), and this sign involves the miraculous production of wine—vast quantities of it. His reputation as an enthusiastic partygoer is certainly at odds with popular conceptions about his followers today—but also with the perceptions of his day as to what constituted proper behaviour, especially for a rabbi. Not only did he like a good celebration (in our 1 December reading he was guest of honour at a dinner party), he was also far from choosy about the company he kept. While the wedding at Cana sounds as if it was a lively community affair, drawing together family, friends and neighbours, as Jesus' ministry developed he became known for going to what we might call the 'wrong sort of parties'. As he told the crowds in the towns of Galilee, 'The Son of Man came eating and drinking, and they say, "Here is a glutton and a drunkard, a friend of tax collectors and sinners"' (Matthew 11:18). While Jesus' cousin, John the Baptist, was renowned for his ascetic lifestyle, the Son of God was notable for enjoying social occasions involving copious quantities of food and drink.

Once again, it is easy to read our own cultural preconceptions into the Cana story. This wasn't a fork buffet followed by an evening disco. Wedding feasts such as the Cana celebration could go on for as long as a week; running out of wine was more than a momentary embarrassment, quickly remedied by a trip to the supermarket. It would be an unforgettable, very public humiliation for the family. As with Mary and the anointing at Bethany, however, Jesus does not give the response that we might expect. While initially seeming to resist his mother's urging to 'do something', he then performs a deed that, to be honest, sounds like something straight out of the adventures of a boy wizard. Instead of telling the host family that they should set their minds on heavenly matters and rejoice in the spiritual blessings of the union, he gathers a team of helpers and draws on his heavenly power to make the best wine that the banqueting master has ever tasted. Already in full swing, the party can now go stratospheric.

Drinking alcohol is not proscribed by the Bible, but we are warned to treat it with respect, to be aware of its potentially destructive consequences. In terms of our personal choices, it is one of those lifestyle issues that Paul would almost certainly have put in the 'meat offered to idols' category (see 1 Corinthians 8 for more on this interesting topic). In short, this means that we should be sensitive to the weakness of our Christian brothers and sisters when exercising our freedom to choose. Paul told the Corinthian believers that they need not worry about eating meat that had been offered to idols. If, however, some found this practice was still damaging to their faith, then it was incumbent on those with less sensitive consciences to refrain out of respect.

Our freedom to drink wine, gin and tonic, or whatever our preferred tipple, should not be exercised in such a way as to create a stumbling block to others. Furthermore, we should never underestimate the ruinous consequences of alcoholism, that addiction which, in its earlier stages, is easily masked by the conventions of our society. Let us thank God for the skill of vine growers, for distillers, for those whose ingenuity can create something that, in its various forms, has given pleasure to many people for many centuries. But let us also pray for all those who suffer the effects of alcohol abuse, whether self-inflicted or inflicted by others, and especially for their protection from harm during this season when merrymaking can tip over into excess.

## For reflection

*'Do not get drunk on wine, which leads to debauchery. Instead, be filled with the Spirit' (Ephesians 5:18).*

*

# MERRYMAKING

Wearing a linen ephod, David was dancing before the Lord with all his might, while he and the entire house of Israel were bringing up the ark of the Lord with shouts and the sound of trumpets. As the ark of the Lord was entering the City of David, Michal daughter of Saul watched from a window. And when she saw King David leaping and dancing before the Lord, she despised him in her heart... When David returned home to bless his household, Michal daughter of Saul came out to meet him and said, 'How the king of Israel has distinguished himself today, going around half-naked in full view of the slave girls of his servants as any vulgar fellow would.' David said to Michal, 'It was before the Lord... I will celebrate before the Lord. I will become even more undignified than this, and I will be humiliated in my own eyes. But by these slave girls you spoke of, I will be held in honour.'

2 SAMUEL 6:14–16, 20–22 (ABRIDGED)

Further along the high street, our pilgrim ears are assailed by raucous music and shrieks of laughter. Yes, it's an office party in full swing and through the steamy windows we glimpse long tables of people in coloured paper hats, firing party poppers, clinking glasses. Two middle-aged men are in full flight in a karaoke duet, eyes closed in mock rapture. Later, so a smiling smoker in the doorway tells us, they'll be pushing back the tables and dancing the hokey-cokey.

Eat, drink and be merry—the history of midwinter merry-making drags in everything from the Roman Saturnalia, the old custom of the Lord of Misrule presiding over the Feast of Fools, the fun and games of the Boy Bishop, even the enduring traditions of the pantomime. As it happens, these various manifestations of apparent lawlessness operated according to strict conventions, so that participants and observers knew where the boundaries were.

The 21st-century office party tends to be hedged around by fewer protocols and behavioural set pieces; nevertheless, it offers an opportunity for loosening of ties, wearing of novelty earrings and socks, letting down of metaphorical hair and (although certainly not in the BRF office) dubious after-hours use of the photocopier.

The celebrations in today's reading were occasioned by an epochal moment for the people of Israel—bringing the ark of the covenant to Jerusalem, which David had only recently established as his capital city, the 'City of David'. The ark was the ceremonial box that held the stone tablets of the law, as given to Moses, and Israel's most sacred symbol of God's covenant and presence with his people. Its arrival in Jerusalem was the culmination of history stretching back to God's promise to Abraham that he would make him into a 'great nation' (see Genesis 12). Some time afterwards, the Lord speaks to David through Nathan the prophet, saying that David's son will build a fitting 'house' (in other words, the temple) for the ark; David's dynasty will be established 'for ever' (2 Samuel 7:16), with the people at rest in the promised land (vv. 10–11).

No wonder David was enthusiastic as he led the worship procession, dancing 'with all his might'. Rather than wearing his kingly robes, he danced in a linen ephod. Now this is not to be confused with the high priest's ephod (see Exodus 28), a kind of multicoloured tabard. What David was wearing was a sleeveless tunic, which was also very, very short. As he leapt and danced, his attire would have left nothing to the imagination. Like traditional wearers of the Scottish kilt, for whom Queen Victoria apparently devised the heavy kilt pin to spare blushes all round in windy Highland weather, the king went *au naturel* beneath his ephod.

David's wife saw and was disgusted. He was the ruler of a victorious, prospering kingdom, yet he was carrying on in front of his people like a 'vulgar fellow'—for full effect, insert your insult of choice. From the perspective of the throne of heaven, though, all earthly rulers are no more than grasshoppers (Isaiah 40:22–23). In the presence of the ark that manifested such majesty, David could not contain his excitement. He was uninhibited in his worship of the Lord, carried away by the drama of the occasion.

The intoxicating effect of Spirit-filled worship was clear on the Day of Pentecost, when some in the watching crowd thought the exhilarated apostles had over-indulged (Acts 2:13). God's presence can produce a dizzying euphoria among his people (although we should note that similar states of ecstasy can be observed among the adherents of other faiths). In more recent times, enthusiastic worship has continued to be characterised by lack of inhibition. Both Shakers and Quakers, for example, were named in mockery of the behaviour observed in their meetings; the tasteful furniture and peace camps came later. In the 1990s, the dramatic manifestations associated with the Toronto Blessing sharply divided Christian opinion as to its appropriateness—waves of spontaneous laughter, animal noises and more. It would seem that the Spirit of God is not overly concerned about our sense of dignity.

Even if we are the kind of person who instinctively shrinks from apparent anarchy (clowns, pantomimes, some forms of charismatic worship), even if we prefer God to speak with a 'still, small voice' (1 Kings 19:12, KJV) rather than with smoke and thunder, let us appreciate the importance of sitting lightly to convention at times, laughing at ourselves and joining with others laughing at themselves. Reading ministerial job adverts, it is fascinating to see how often churches require a 'sense of humour' in their leader, besides the usual preaching and pastoral skills. We are all human and we all make mistakes and there are times when we need our leaders to be merciful, to laugh forgivingly and tell us, 'That's OK, don't worry about it'—and to be able to laugh at themselves, too.

When the usual conventions are relaxed and the established order is in disarray, whether at an office party or through a dramatic movement of the Holy Spirit, we face the possibility of change, which is always a sign of life, uncomfortable though the process may be. An unexpectedly apposite example of this is the two-part Christmas Special of *The Office* (2003), the comedy 'mockumentary' by Ricky Gervais and Stephen Merchant. The assorted characters are brought together for their annual party, and, as events unfold, crises develop and are resolved, cruelty receives its come-uppance, love is fulfilled and truth is told. Just about everybody emerges changed in some way by their experiences.

What should characterise our merrymaking? Whether our gatherings are lively, night-long affairs or two couples enjoying each other's company for an hour or so, we can delight in laughter, hospitality, in not taking ourselves too seriously, seeking always to include rather than exclude, to affirm and build up rather than undermine and pull down.

Remembering that Jesus loved a good party, we can also be mindful of his presence with us, if we are tempted to push the boundaries too far and to embrace disorder in a way that we will later regret.

## For reflection

'A merry heart doeth good like a medicine' (Proverbs 17:22, KJV).

✳

## 5 December

# UNDER THE MISTLETOE

Let him kiss me with the kisses of his mouth—for your love is more delightful than wine. Pleasing is the fragrance of your perfumes; your name is like perfume poured out. No wonder the young women love you! Take me away with you—let us hurry! Let the king bring me into his chambers... My beloved spoke and said to me, 'Arise, my darling, my beautiful one, come with me. See! The winter is past; the rains are over and gone. Flowers appear on the earth; the season of singing has come, the cooing of doves is heard in our land. The fig-tree forms its early fruit; the blossoming vines spread their fragrance. Arise, come, my darling; my beautiful one, come with me.'

SONG OF SONGS 1:2–4; 2:10–13

Leaving the party behind (some of us with a thankful shudder, others with envious backward glances—winter dusk is falling and the wind promises drizzle), we thread our way between the late afternoon shoppers and almost fall over a couple emerging from a darkened doorway. Their faces are flushed, there is lipstick on his collar, and her blouse is in considerable disarray. He wears a wedding ring; she does not. As they attempt to slip back discreetly into the party restaurant, they are greeted by a chorus of wolf whistles. This is where the shadow side of Christmas misrule can reveal itself, when fantasy opportunities for rewriting life's script

33

present themselves. Some will dream that those suggestive text messages, the covert glances over the water cooler and that lingering conversation in the post room could turn out to be an escape route from whatever mess and inconvenience are left behind at home each morning.

At the same time, for many people the Christmas season seems to hold out a promise that the coming year will bring the long-dreamed-of, hitherto elusive, true love. Whether or not our faith will permit us a residual belief in the efficacy of mistletoe, kissing under the golden bough is only traditional, isn't it? Richard Curtis's unashamedly feel-good Christmas film *Love Actually* (2003) presented a cross-section of stories, each exploring a different experience of love—unrequited, newly married, unexpected, adulterous, fraternal and so on. Like a subterranean echo, the fear that reverberates beneath is that of the solitary Christmas, the Day spent alone, contemplating the lack of a significant other to provide the lifeblood of love and friendship.

Today's reading is from that part of scripture dear to the heart of so many youth group Bible studies. The Song of Songs is unequivocally erotic, a series of poems conveying the earthshaking experience of passionate human love and deep mutual sexual attraction, revelling in graphic imagery that our English translations struggle to convey with due decorum. The best efforts of generations of biblical inter-pretation fail to convince that the poems are chiefly descriptive of the love between Christ and his Church (a relationship that is, admittedly, described in terms of marriage by a number of biblical writers: see Ephesians 5:25–27, for example).

Reading our chosen passage in December may evoke mental images of a cartoon springtime bursting out all over, of flowers unfolding from the beloved's footprints, bluebirds trilling from the blossoming cherry trees. Yet anybody who has ever fallen in love can affirm that this is pretty much how it feels. The emotions are literally enchanting, transporting us to what seems like a fairytale realm, where nothing bad will happen to us ever again. There is danger in enchantment, though, as any fairytale princess can tell. If we make the wrong choice, if we fail to reflect on the consequences of our actions, we just might find ourselves turned to stone, transmuted into a frog or facing some similarly unpleasant fate. The flames of passion can bring a brighter illumination to life than we could have imagined possible, yet, if we are careless in how we let them burn, they may reduce our lives—and the lives of others—to dust and ashes.

We should never be tempted to deny or play down the strength of erotic and romantic love. The God-given boundaries for such love—within the mutually binding vows of a lifelong and committed relationship—mean that its voltage can be harnessed and held back from becoming destructive. As with alcohol (and, as many know to their cost, alcohol and sexual attraction are an explosive combination), we must treat it with great care, respecting its power. The Song of Songs voice identified as 'She' warns her friends, the 'daughters of Jerusalem' (8:4), 'do not arouse or awaken love until it so desires'.

There is a deeper significance to the springtime imagery, however. It can speak to us of renewal, of green shoots emerging from that which seemed long dead. We may feel that we are without hope in our personal relationships, that our best chance of happiness is in plotting a way out, because we deserve something—or rather, someone—better. Such an attitude tends to be the assumption of too many media columnists, screenplay writers and confessional authors. By contrast, our God (for whom, as Jesus assured us, 'all things are possible': Matthew 19:26) can bring new hope and life as unstoppable as springtime to the most wintry of relationships, if both parties are committed to the necessary, at times exhausting spadework in the garden of love.

With respect to those for whom the fear of Christmas alone is a painful and present reality, no glib solutions should be offered. If we are blessed with a loving companion of our own, we should hold back from telling others how they ought to focus on the positive, be thankful for small mercies and reflect on whether they are in fact called to singleness, to do great works for the kingdom. All the while, much as they love the Lord, they may be longing for a different, human love—one 'with skin on', as the saying goes.

The family of the Church must be characterised by listening to each other's deepest emotions, hurts and needs, and by caring for one another beyond the call of duty. We must love our brothers and sisters in Christ with a costly, self-giving love, expressed in a fellowship that is genuinely accessible to all, whatever their economic, marital or social status. This love is that of which Paul wrote so powerfully in 1 Corinthians 13—the 'most excellent way' (12:31)—and it is the ultimate healing offered by God to his longing, lonely world.

## For reflection

*'Love is as strong as death, its jealousy as unyielding as the grave. It burns like blazing fire, like a mighty flame. Many waters cannot quench love; rivers cannot sweep it away. If one were to give all the wealth of one's house for love, it would be utterly scorned'* (Song of Songs 8:6b–7).

*

*6 December*

# SANTA

[Jesus said] 'So I say to you: ask and it will be given to you; seek and you will find; knock and the door will be opened to you. For everyone who asks receives; those who seek find; and to those who knock, the door will be opened. Which of you fathers, if your son asks for a fish, will give him a snake instead? Or if he asks for an egg, will give him a scorpion? If you then, though you are evil, know how to give good gifts to your children, how much more will your Father in heaven give the Holy Spirit to those who ask him!'
LUKE 11:9–13

At the top of the high street, our pilgrimage takes us to press our noses against the Christmas window displays of what is still a family-run department store, a classic of its kind where you can choose between three kinds of clothes pegs, buy slippers and school uniforms, find a cover for the patio furniture and visit Santa's grotto, with its bodyguard of life-sized animatronic reindeer. Children will be encouraged to climb on the knee of a heavily bearded stranger and whisper their Christmas present wish list in his ear. Some will have nightmares for weeks afterwards; others will look back on the experience with nostalgia, especially if their fathers compound the wonder by appearing in the living room in Santa attire on Christmas morning. My maternal grandfather maintained this tradition for his five children, a tradition now remembered by my mother chiefly for the year when he accidentally set his false beard alight by leaning too close to the candlelit Christmas tree.

Today is the feast day of St Nicholas (in Dutch *Sinte Klaas*, hence Santa Claus), commemorating the Bishop of Myra in what is now Turkey. The saint was born in the late third century at Patara on the southern coast, also known today for its long sandy beach and breeding colony of sea turtles. Somehow or other, a revered ecclesiastical leader from a hot Mediterranean country ended up as patron saint of—in effect—the North Pole, a clinically obese old man in a fur-trimmed red suit (colour largely determined by a long-ago series of Coca-Cola adverts), who annually performs a magical compression of time and space to deliver gifts to children around the globe, if possible via their chimneys. Recently, a new pilgrimage tradition has arisen at this time of year, whereby parents save up to take children to Lapland—or a virtual Lapland set up somewhere in a UK pine forest—where I gather they meet the saint himself, amid appropriate elves, ice and snow.

Some may be surprised to discover that Father Christmas has any basis in fact whatsoever, that he is more than another childhood myth, on a par with the bogeyman and the tooth fairy—but there he is in the Church calendar, admittedly as St Nicholas rather than any of his more recent, fanciful incarnations. With such an imprimatur, we should assume that we can gain valuable insights from what we know of his life, and not just about the importance of, say, keeping to budget when shopping for presents.

When reflecting on the lives of saints, including those who lived far more recently than Nicholas, it can be very hard to disentangle stories grounded in substance from those written by a posthumous fan club with the fervent and understandable desire to build a bigger and better reputation for their man or woman. There is little doubt, though, that in his lifetime the original Nicholas was known not only for the strength of his faith, proved through suffering, but also for his generosity.

Imprisoned and tortured by the Roman authorities in Myra during one of the waves of persecution that battered the Church in its early centuries, Bishop Nicholas was released when Constantine became Emperor, and was present at the Council of Nicaea in 325. While there, he apparently ended up in serious trouble for slapping the face of the Egyptian priest Arius, who had denied Jesus' equality with God the Father. Nicholas's own parents had been very wealthy and, when they both died in a plague epidemic while he was still only in his mid-teens, he set himself to dispose of their wealth wisely. Many stories were told of his generosity with both money and possessions, as he dedicated himself to helping the poor and needy.

One episode involved a man so poor that he was unable to provide any kind of dowry for his three daughters, which meant that they were unlikely to marry well, if at all. Even worse, it seemed probable that he would be forced to sell them into slavery. In the midst of his despair, a miracle occurred, three times over. On three different occasions, a bag of gold appeared in the house, thrown through an open window to land in stockings or shoes left before the fire to dry. Not only did the gold provide for the daughters' dowries but, over time, a custom arose whereby children hung out stockings or put out shoes in the hope that the saint would fill them.

St Nicholas is best known as patron saint of children and another popular story recounts how he brought back to life three boys (in some versions of the story they are identified as theological students) who had been murdered and pickled by a particularly nasty local shopkeeper in Myra. The popular medieval ceremony of appointing a Boy Bishop would often take place on St Nicholas' day, ecclesiastical pomp and dignity submitting to subversion by a small and quite possibly cheeky chorister until 28 December.

We began this week thinking about presents, and how our Christmas giving echoes the breathtaking generosity of the Father towards us. Our Bible passage today directs us to examine our own instinctive generosity to children, whether our own or others who are precious to us (and, however tight the finances, most parents gladly stint themselves to give the family 'a good Christmas'), thereby deepening our appreciation of how God can delight in pouring out for us his very self—living water, bread of life. St Nicholas is remembered now because of the generous spirit that he embodied, but, rather than simply linking him with seasonal giving, we can reflect on him as an example of one so devoted to serving God that the Spirit coursed through his life unchecked, touching with grace all those he encountered.

The presence of the Spirit within us and within our churches creates a culture of liberality, where selfless and reciprocal giving becomes instinctive, an automatic response in every area of being and doing. This means that we can ask in the confidence of a courteous, rather than curt, response; we are unafraid to seek because we trust that we will be guided to what we need; we knock in the expectation of a warm welcome. Such a community can provide the true sense of family that so many long to find, offering the affirmation and acceptance for which they may otherwise search in vain. Such a community will bless all who belong to it—and will draw others to the kingdom more surely than the most eloquent of evangelistic sermons.

## For reflection

*'Give, and it will be given to you. A good measure, pressed down, shaken together and running over, will be poured into your lap. For with the measure you use, it will be measured to you'* (Luke 6:38).

*

## 7 December

# 'TOMORROW WE DIE'

There is a time for everything, and a season for every activity under the heavens: a time to be born and a time to die, a time to plant and a time to uproot, a time to kill and a time to heal, a time to tear down and a time to build, a time to weep and a time to laugh, a time to mourn and a time to dance, a time to scatter stones and a time to gather them, a time to embrace and a time to refrain, a time to search and a time to give up, a time to keep and a time to throw away, a time to tear and a time to mend, a time to be silent and a time to speak, a time to love and a time to hate, a time for war and a time for peace.

ECCLESIASTES 3:1–8

We come to the end of the beginning of our pilgrimage, and our journey has brought us to the edge of the city centre. We stand now on a bridge, heads bowed beneath the streetlights, looking at a roadside shrine of drooping flowers in cellophane and a few scribbled cards of sympathy. Somebody has died here, their life cut short by a careless driver; somebody's Christmas presents will remain unopened and there will be a gap at the dinner table.

We have reflected on 'Eat, drink and be merry' but that phrase has a sober ending: 'for tomorrow we die'. An example of a *memento mori* (the Latin for 'remember you must die'), it is found in the Bible (see Isaiah 22:13; also 1 Corinthians

15:32 and Jesus' parable of the rich fool in Luke 12:16–21) and, over the centuries, it has remained a popular motif for poets, painters and philosophers.

As this famous passage from Ecclesiastes reminds us, a time comes when the party is over and we are walking home in the dark. Equally, a time comes when the crumbling tower block is demolished and chic new flats rise from the rubble. A baby is born, first of the next generation, and brings joy and exhaustion in equal measure to his parents. An elderly brother and sister pick up the phone and speak for the first time in years, and wonder what took them so long. A cyclist forgets to check behind as he changes lanes on the bridge— and his life is cut short by the bus he didn't know was there.

Given the inevitability of change in our cosmos, it is curious how often people speak of it in troubled, even fearful tones. A baleful chorus of 'nobody likes change' accompanies the efforts of too many church leaders, for example, as they attempt the mind-bending task of 'keeping the existing congregation happy' while 'attracting young families'. Change is associated with uncertainty, instability, loss of meaning, even when the majority view is that it is change for the better. The film *Goodbye Lenin* (2003) summarised this perspective with subtlety and humour in the story of a grown-up son shielding his mother from any knowledge of the 1989 East German regime change—even to the extent of buying up outdated newspapers and food in familiar packaging, lest the turmoil of discovery undermine her already weakened health.

The *memento mori* forcefully reminds us that not only is change unavoidable, but it brings pain as well as blessing, sorrow as well as smiles. Night follows day; at the end of life is death, whether long-anticipated or brutally unexpected. The path to the church may lead through a graveyard. Rather than facing up to the fears that such reflection may stir up within us, however, it is tempting to keep talking, keep walking, refuse to stop and think in case our fragile sense of security starts to crumble in the silence.

Our culture has a prevailing fear of silence, according to author Sara Maitland. In her powerful exploration of the subject, *A Book of Silence*, she describes sensing a wholly unexpected call to pursue a life of solitude and silence (unexpected, she points out, given her gregarious upbringing and love of conversation). Spending time in a number of remote cottages, ending with a sense of homecoming among the high moors of northern Galloway, she describes unspeakable joys, moments of sheer terror but always a sense of journey, away from superficial distractions and deeper into the presence of God.

Writing of a night of vigil in the Sinai desert, she says:

*I conceived a vast, lovely and awestruck sense of God. God, in this desert context, does not say be safe, be cosy, here's a woolly blanket, a tidy cocoon, a place of refuge... Love your life and you'll lose it. Risk it and maybe, just, you'll totter into heaven—the place of both annihilation and total knowledge, the place of beauty and joy. The risk is absolute; you'll get nothing else out of it, not pleasure, not health, not affection, not comfort and certainly not safety. Just the beauty of God.* [3]

For her, choosing silence was a way through fear of loss of meaning into a place where she could begin to glimpse the implications of eternity.

Space and silence are what some people require to process what they think and feel about themselves and about their faith. Others need to talk things through with somebody else to get their heads round a decision or an issue. Whatever our personal preference, it is good to make opportunities from time to time to think about our lives in a wider perspective, whether with friends in the pub after work or on a monastic retreat. Advent offers a good excuse for such reflection, playing a similar role to Lent in the Church calendar as the fast before the feast, the gathering darkness before the coming of the light, and a time for meditating on Christ's second coming at the end of time.

Looking again at our passage from Ecclesiastes, we can understand its rhythm as actually bestowing blessing rather than threat. We may long for good times to last for ever, but surely part of their goodness is that they help to strengthen us for the next stage of our journey through life, which may well bring hardship. When we are going through hardship, we can perceive how change might once again be a means of blessing, because we have the assurance that pain and suffering do not last for ever either, no matter how bleak our prospects may seem at the moment.

Our mortal selves are too frail for the infinite spaces of time-no-longer; we can endure only for a limited season. We have a huge and holy hope to sustain us, though, far greater than the knowledge that both good times and bad times will pass. We have the hope of 'death swallowed up in victory', in the words of Paul (see 1 Corinthians 15:54). In the death and resurrection of Jesus, we have the sign that one day, on the other side of the grave, we too will be raised to new and eternal life, and all tears will be dried and every heart consoled, for ever.

## For reflection

*Spend some time meditating on these words of Jesus: 'I am the resurrection and the life. Anyone who believes in me will live, even though they die; and whoever lives by believing in me will never die. Do you believe this?' (John 11:25–26).*

# Earn all you can, save all you can, give all you can

As our second week of pilgrimage begins, we find ourselves in a most respectable neighbourhood in the city suburbs. Pilgrims may spend more than a few nights in sleeping bags on church hall floors, but the residents round here must surely sleep more comfortably. The houses are old and substantial, some gentrified to the latest specifications, others having the look of not-so-much-smart-as-comfortable family home. The lives of these locals have turned out well, on the whole, and their expectation is that their children's lives will turn out the same. They certainly know how to 'eat, drink and be merry' and, like everything else they do, they tend to make a good show of it.

Pilgrimage involves coming to a greater understanding of ourselves as well as learning about the places through which we journey, and in these next seven days we move beyond considering how we celebrate the Christmas season to reflecting on the values that underpin what we do. Perhaps we aspire to ordering our lives in line with the latest 'personal development' theories, making sure that every part of who we are and what we do is appropriately focused and purposeful; perhaps we simply try to be good, according to the Golden Rule learnt in a long-ago Sunday school class. We may be the sort to commend ourselves for our recycling prowess and our personal Fair Trade credentials; or we have the regular pleasure of applauding as our family members collect sporting trophies, music certificates and academic scholarships. We may be leaders of a church surfing the crest of the popularity wave, as crowds jostle for a seat at one of the packed services on our roster.

Whatever our circumstances, it is always helpful to pause periodically and ask ourselves, 'Why?' Why do we value this and do that? Do we, for example, put sporting achievement ahead of regular commitment to our local church? Or do we find it beyond comprehension that any 'proper Christian' might not vote the same way as us in a General Election? If we found ourselves face to face with Jesus, what would he say about our set of working assumptions about what really matters? Would we emerge from the encounter any better than the Pharisees, whom he derided as 'whitewashed tombs' (Matthew 23:27)? The unavoidable biblical imperative is that we should never stop seeking to bring our lives under the searching gaze of God—and he always moves ahead of us, calling us to follow, showing us the way through what John Bunyan called 'the wilderness of this world'.

*8 December*

# MORE AND MORE AND MORE

Those who love money never have enough; those who love wealth are never satisfied with their income... As goods increase, so do those who consume them. And what benefit are they to the owners except to feast their eyes on them? The sleep of labourers is sweet, whether they eat little or much, but the abundance of the rich permits them no sleep. I have seen a grievous evil under the sun: wealth hoarded to the harm of its owners, or wealth lost through some misfortune, so that when they have children there is nothing left for them to inherit. Everyone comes naked from their mother's womb, and as everyone comes, so they depart. They take nothing from their toil that they can carry in their hands. This too is a grievous evil: As everyone comes, so they depart, and what do they gain, since they toil for the wind? All their days they eat in darkness, with great frustration, affliction and anger.

ECCLESIASTES 5:10–17 (ABRIDGED)

The enormous detached house on the corner plot, with a glimpse of sumptuous garden, is definitely the house of a rich person, somebody wealthy by most people's standards. Maybe this is where a hedge fund manager retreats to enjoy the rewards of their financial wizardry—or possibly a captain of industry or a public servant of the first order. These days, many communities around the UK include swathes of men and women who did not inherit wealth but now enjoy a level of affluence and material comfort that was unimaginable to previous generations. The achievement of such wealth tends, rightly or wrongly, to bring enhanced social status and a presumption of what some would term 'wisdom' but should be described more correctly as expertise. 'They must be pretty clever at what they do,' onlookers might say. 'They've certainly done well out of it.'

The difficulty with wealth is knowing when enough is enough, and it is much harder to hold on to a concept of 'enough' when we live in a country where economic health is measured by credit-fuelled continuous growth and year-on-year profit increases. Our duty as good citizens is to buy and keep on buying, to shop for Britain. When we find more or less everything affordable, it may well be hard to say 'no' to ourselves and especially to those for whom we are responsible. We don't have to buy paint from the local DIY centre, because we can afford to decorate our conservatory in hand-mixed Georgian hues. Now that each of our children has a TV, we can think about one of those home cinema systems. We can holiday abroad every year, thanks to cheap flights, so why not go twice? Three times?

Our Bible passage bluntly points out that we need a right attitude to wealth. It is so easy to become enslaved by wanting it, by attaining it, and then by worrying about its potential loss. We tell ourselves that we do not love riches for their own sake, that we are not misers hoarding sacks of gold in the back bedroom; we simply want to provide for our families. Without realising it, however, we may have ended up being controlled by our wealth rather than controlling it. The final verse from our Ecclesiastes passage may not ring true until we think of the mind-boggling commutes to the office that so many workers endure, day after day. They rise in the dark and return after dark (especially in winter), quite possibly 'with great frustration, affliction and anger' if they have failed to get a seat on the train home.

Apart from the way in which it can enslave our hearts, wealth can be toxic because we start to forget where it ultimately came from. We may come to believe that we have prospered entirely due to the work of our own hands, and forget to give thanks and ascribe honour where it is due. Worse, we can start to consider all that we have as our exclusive property, to dispose of entirely as we please, to benefit only ourselves and our blood relatives and close friends. The Old Testament laws, with their pattern of sabbaths and jubilees, were given precisely to safeguard God's people against such attitudes: 'You may say to yourself, "My power and the strength of my hands have produced this wealth for me." But remember the Lord your God, for it is he who gives you this ability to produce wealth' (Deuteronomy 8:17–18).

Wrongly handled, riches can indeed make it hard for us to enter the kingdom of heaven, as Jesus warned (see Mark 10:23–25), because they encourage us to assume that we lack nothing—or that if we notice any kind of lack, we can always buy something to sort out the problem. Perhaps, therefore, it would be best if we simply gave everything away and lived by faith, trusting for God's provision as the prophet Elijah did (1 Kings 17:2–6). Who knows but that stray ravens may drop loaves and steak on our doorsteps?

Contrary to the assumptions of some parts of the Church, though, there is no unified biblical line on the subject of wealth. There is no unequivocal command to get rid of it, but there is plenty of teaching about good stewardship of what we have been given and the importance of exercising our responsibilities wisely, always being mindful of those who have less than we do. And that can only happen if we have our priorities in order, however much or little we are worth in financial terms.

As Jesus points out, in one of the better-known Gospel verses, 'No one can serve two masters. Either you will hate the one and love the other, or you will be devoted to the one and despise the other. You cannot serve both God and Money' (Matthew 6:24). If we are wealthy, we can serve God with our wealth, using our influence to further the causes of the kingdom. Turning again to *A Christmas Carol*, it is interesting to note that while Ebenezer Scrooge is made a new man by his encounters with the three Spirits of Christmas, he remains rich—but he becomes kind and munificent, for the rest of his life taking enormous pleasure by surprising others with his charity.

In global terms, of course, every one of us who can afford to buy this book qualifies as rich. Part of developing a rightful sense of 'enough' is ensuring that we maintain at least some awareness of the wealth and poverty of the wider world. Social commentators point out that those who live in societies marked by substantial inequality of income are more likely to exhibit dissatisfaction and frustration, as one group compares its lot with those higher up the economic scale. We need to look beyond our own shores and train ourselves to think in terms of global inequalities. That way, our ears will be readier to detect God's guidance as to what we should do with all that he has entrusted to us. Then, money will be our servant, not our master.

## *Prayer*

*Lord God, give us grateful hearts for the riches with which you have blessed us. May our lives be characterised by generosity and our hearts not constrained by envy of others. Grant insight and thoughtfulness to those who have more, that they may use it wisely and well.*

## 9 December

# TOGETHER WE CAN OVERCOME

Blessed are those whose ways are blameless, who walk according to the law of the Lord. Blessed are those who keep his statutes and seek him with all their heart—they do no wrong but follow his ways. You have laid down precepts that are to be fully obeyed. Oh, that my ways were steadfast in obeying your decrees! Then I would not be put to shame when I consider all your commands. I will praise you with an upright heart as I learn your righteous laws. I will obey your decrees; do not utterly forsake me. How can those who are young keep their way pure? By living according to your word. I seek you with all my heart; do not let me stray from your commands. I have hidden your word in my heart that I might not sin against you.
PSALM 119:1–11

Next door to the house of riches, we find a very contrasting dwelling. This one is of the not-so-much-smart-as-comfortable types, a big shambling house, unmarked by 21st-century standards of renovation. If we look closely, we glimpse the hint of a much-faded mural on the side wall, from a past decade before the neighbourhood was gentrified. The window stickers in the middle-aged cars parked in the driveway suggest that these are people who care deeply about the environment; they campaign on behalf of the downtrodden; they are anti-elitist, pro-egalitarian, full of youthful zeal even if, for some of them, youth is a distant memory.

The events of recent decades have failed to prove that political activism alone can set society on a path of permanent and unimpeded improvement. In 2008, the media were filled with reminiscences about the student protest movements of 40 years before. Columnists opined as to what had happened to all that ardour, that belief that the world could be changed for the better by lots of placard-waving and shouting. The 1989 revolutions in Eastern Europe, ending more than 50 years of Communist rule, felt like a truly new dawn and Francis Fukuyama's slogan 'the end of history' was much bandied about; at last the Cold War was finished and we could all move on. In country after country, so it seemed, the people simply had to get together, ring bells, sing hymns, and the government troops laid down their weapons and the state relinquished power. But any illusions as to the limitless possibilities of the peacemaking and cooperation now unleashed were dashed by the outbreak of war and the ensuing genocidal atrocities in the countries that were formerly part of Yugoslavia.

Politics tends to be in the business of promising better worlds and brave new hopes. The British Labour Party victory in 1997 felt like another hugely significant moment for many who had grown up under Conservative rule, but the years of government that followed inevitably brought disappointment and a sense of promises broken or kept in letter rather than spirit. By mid-2009, the public perception of the entire UK political establishment, of whatever party persuasion, reached a nadir with the weeks of scandal over Parliamentary expenses. It would seem that higher moral and ethical agendas are easily forgotten when individuals get a whiff of a free lunch (or toilet seat, mortgage tax relief or moat maintenance).

Our reading today takes the opening verses of the longest psalm in the Bible. Psalm 119 is an extended meditation on God's law, both the words of guidance given for daily life and God's promised rewards, linked to obedience to his law. The constant refrain is that true happiness and true wisdom can come only through following God's way. The psalmist knows that youthful energy and enthusiasm (v. 9) are all very well, but, unless we continue to seek the Lord's presence, letting his righteousness sink deep into our hearts, our efforts will end up as futile, at best. Without his guidance, we will stumble and fall in the dark, as the vivid imagery of a well-known later verse in the same psalm makes clear: 'Your word is a lamp to my feet and a light for my path' (v. 105).

That particular verse has often been taught as a 'memory verse' about how Christians should value the Bible, but it is thought-provoking that, in this psalm, the focus is on delighting in God's law. In Hebrew, this is *Torah*, which primarily denotes the first five books of the Old Testament (Genesis, Exodus, Leviticus, Numbers and Deuteronomy), parts of which are probably among the least-read chapters of scripture nowadays. We can use it as a reminder that, while we are children of Christ's new covenant, our faith should be informed by the whole of scripture, not only our favourite bits from the Gospels and epistles, with a psalm or three thrown in.

Reading and reflecting on the chequered history of God's people in the books of Kings and Chronicles, for example, offers many salutary stories of the inadequacy of human versus God-given wisdom, which can inform our opinions about the interrelationship of faith and political action. In the final days of the kingdom of Judah, the very survival of Jerusalem, the capital city, depended on the authorities choosing the right strategy towards their foreign overlords. The prophet Jeremiah had the terrible task of bringing God's guidance to Zedekiah, who would turn out to be the last king of Judah. It would be better (said Jeremiah) to surrender to the Babylonians—who had, after all, put Zedekiah on the throne—than continue to rebel. Predictably and sadly, the king refused and the ensuing catastrophe for both king and people is recounted in Jeremiah 39.

It is vital to have Christians involved at all levels in the political life of a nation, so long as nobody falls under the illusion of thinking that it is possible to legislate a perfect world into existence. Better, yes, but not perfect, because however well-informed and well-intentioned our plans, they can only operate within a human context, within the limits enforced by our shaky virtue and unshakeable selfishness. We may like to believe that enough cooperation and dialogue can overcome any obstacle, but while these ways of working are helpful in themselves, they do not solve the fundamental problem of the wayward human heart.

As we have already considered, Advent is the season when we look forward to Christ's promised return, when 'the earth will be filled with the knowledge of the glory of the Lord as the waters cover the sea' (Habakkuk 2:14). While we work and wait in this in-between time, we can follow the psalmist's example and soak our minds in the ways of God and the values of his kingdom. We submit our plans to his guiding hand and, whatever earthly position of authority we may hold, we never forget to acknowledge the heavenly source from which all power and authority are derived.

## For reflection

'God exalted him to the highest place and gave him the name that is above every name, that at the name of Jesus every knee should bow, in heaven and on earth and under the earth, and every tongue acknowledge that Jesus Christ is Lord, to the glory of God the Father' (Philippians 2:9–11).

*10 December*

# KEEPING THE RULES

Meanwhile, the elder son was in the field. When he came near the house, he heard music and dancing. So he called one of the servants and asked him what was going on. 'Your brother has come,' he replied, 'and your father has killed the fattened calf because he has him back safe and sound.' The elder brother became angry and refused to go in. So his father went out and pleaded with him. But he answered his father, 'Look! All these years I've been slaving for you and never disobeyed your orders. Yet you never gave me even a young goat so I could celebrate with my friends. But when this son of yours who has squandered your property with prostitutes comes home, you kill the fattened calf for him!' 'My son,' the father said, 'you are always with me, and everything I have is yours. But we had to celebrate and be glad, because this brother of yours was dead and is alive again; he was lost and is found.'

LUKE 15:25–32

At the very next house we reach, we don't have time to note the size of the building, the state of the garden or the quality of the cars on the driveway, because the door is opened wide, welcoming in the weary pilgrims. This is the home of a good person—a woman, as it happens—one of the first to sign the local church rota to provide hospitality along the way. The woodstove is glowing; the rugs are soft, the mince pies warm (but not microwaved until scalding in the middle), the wine mulled.

This woman is one of those people who oil the wheels of neighbourhood life, who pay their subs on time and volunteer to be school governors, members of the church council or coordinators of the fête committee. They are known for putting others first, for always being ready to help, even if it involves tedious chores. At school they were picked as prefects and may have risen to the heights of head boy or girl. The unkind and the naturally indolent might murmur 'Busybody', but these people simply want to do their bit to keep things running smoothly. If we don't recognise ourselves in them, we probably know somebody who fits the bill.

Yesterday we touched on the importance of getting to know the whole Bible well; today's reading, from Jesus' parable of the lost son (also know as the prodigal son), illustrates the danger of focusing on a few favourite passages. They may become so familiar that we cease to perceive the force of their message, which sometimes goes so far as to be downright offensive to those who assume (not least on the basis of society's reassurance) that they are good people. Take the story of Martha and Mary (Luke 10:38–42), in which Jesus commends Mary, who sits at his feet and listens, rather than Martha, the overworked hostess. A vicar told me recently that when he read that passage to a group who were completely new to faith, their reaction was unexpected. Without prior knowledge that Mary's example was supposed to be the correct one, they were annoyed at Jesus' unfairness by not appearing to value Martha's contribution—which would, of course, have been the reaction of the original witnesses to the event.

Most relatively well-taught Christians know that the

elder son emerges least favourably from today's parable, compared with the forgiving father and the penitent son, and we are not likely to want to identify with this character. Bible teaching tends to linger on the warmth of the father's loving embrace for the returned runaway (a popular image for Christian book covers), encouraging the hearers to do likewise and thus overlook the true ending of the story, which is somewhat less comforting. In fact, it contains a profound rebuke for anybody who has ever felt confident that they know the full measure of our heavenly Father's grace, that it is a straightforward matter to decide who has 'made it' through the narrow gate leading to kingdom life (see Matthew 7:13–14) and who has most definitely not.

Let's try to recover the shock of this parable's conclusion. The elder son has been a model child. Rather than following his brother's example and leaving as soon as he received his share of the inheritance (the father 'divided his property between them', v. 12), he stayed to work on the family land. It is quite likely that he had to work harder than before, because of his younger brother's absence. Indeed, he was toiling in the fields while the loving reunion of father and son occurred, and it sounds as if nobody thought to summon him home early as the party preparations got underway. Then he comes in, hot and tired, and finds not only that his disgraced brother is allowed back into the home but that a lavish celebration is taking place.

Jesus told this story, and also two earlier ones about lost sheep and coins (see 15:3–7, 8–10), as a rebuke to 'the Pharisees and the teachers of the law' (v. 2) who were angry at the way he welcomed and even broke bread with the social pariahs of the day. Jesus was addressing the ones who were the good people, not only in their own eyes but in the perception of their community, the ones who knew the covenant law inside out and devoted themselves to getting it right. His message was, by contrast, about the limitless expanse and unmerited riches of grace.

An even more outrageous example of God's apparent unfairness is Jesus' story of the workers in the vineyard (Matthew 20:1–16). Those who have laboured all day are paid the same amount as those who have worked just one hour, and when they complain to the owner of the vineyard, his response takes no account of what we would deem proportionality: '"Don't I have the right to do what I want with my own money? Or are you envious because I am generous?"' (v. 15).

Such generosity and grace carry enormous risks. The gift can be rudely snatched and the giver despised. The runaway younger son might wake up one morning feeling that the farm really is too boring after all—and, this time, he takes off with his brother's inheritance as well. The vineyard workers might look down on those who were stupid enough to end up working through the heat of the day, rather than being grateful for the wages they had received. Mary might decide never to lift a finger to help Martha ever again—hadn't she got Jesus' authorisation for a more laidback lifestyle?

Those risks are part of the scandal of grace, with which Paul memorably wrestled in his letter to the church in Rome: 'Shall we go on sinning, so that grace may increase? By no means!' (Romans 6:1–2). The truth is indisputable, however: we cannot earn salvation, whoever we are and whatever we do. We may know ourselves to be like the kind woman we encountered at the start of today's reading: our good works undoubtedly help to make the world a better place, and that is undoubtedly an excellent thing. We must remember, though, that God's love is unconditional. Salvation is his free gift, held out to absolutely everyone with no exceptions. Once we have accepted the gift and become part of God's family, his Spirit continues to transform us into the likeness of Christ ('sanctify' being the good old-fashioned word for this), but the Father never has favourites. At the heavenly banquet, a bishop will not have a better seat than a penitent paedophile.

## For prayer

*As a response, we can use the words of the Jesus Prayer, derived from the cry of a blind beggar seeking healing (Mark 10:47): 'Lord Jesus Christ, Son of God, have mercy on me, a sinner'.*

*

## *11 December*

# HAPPY FAMILY CHRISTMAS

Then Jesus entered a house, and again a crowd gathered, so
that he and his disciples were not even able to eat. When his
family heard about this, they went to take charge of him, for
they said, 'He is out of his mind.' … Standing outside, they
sent someone in to call him. A crowd was sitting round him,
and they told him, 'Your mother and brothers are outside
looking for you.' 'Who are my mother and my brothers?' he
asked. Then he looked at those seated in a circle round him
and said, 'Here are my mother and my brothers! Whoever does
God's will is my brother and sister and mother.'
MARK 3:20–21, 31–35 (ABRIDGED)

As well as chestnuts roasting on an open fire and ample
silent snowfall (not a howling blizzard), the perfect fantasy
Christmas involves some kind of extended family scenario.
The clan gathers, every possible dispute peaceably resolved
about who is going to stay with whom and who will do
the cooking. Nobody sulks or carps; there are no vicious
undercurrents or crackling tensions. But when real families
get together, our illusions about one another can be shattered,
and as a result the new year is heralded by a massive rise in
people initiating divorce proceedings. A festive drink in the
last-chance saloon turns into the final straw…

If, on our Advent pilgrimage, we lingered in this nice
neighbourhood until the festive day itself, we would not

have to search far before we encountered both positive and negative sides of the family Christmas. A quick walk down the road will yield, on one side, the view of an extended family sitting down for a late lunch, chatting, laughing and nodding as plates of delicious food are passed down the table. Even the teenagers are smiling and Granny and Grandpa sit, fully *compos mentis*, at the head and foot of the table.

Meanwhile, on the other side of the road, a man slams his car door and starts up the engine, revving furiously. A woman leans out of a ground-floor window, smudged mascara on her cheeks, and shouts an injunction to leave that is unprintable in a BRF book. The living room is lit only by the cold, flickering light of a TV and, faintly, we can detect the snarl of small children fighting over electronic gaming devices, and a whiff of burnt potatoes. So which of these two families would we describe as more 'biblical'?

We may never have questioned our assumption that 'family values' are part of the bedrock of the Christian faith, and it is certainly true that both Old and New Testaments show us a society centred on the tribal clan, linked by birth and intermarriage. Throughout biblical history, the culture was generally far more family-centred than ours: as in pre-Industrial Revolution England, the family unit was the basis of economic life rather than a haven for retreat from the world. That is the context for Jesus' eye-poppingly dismissive remarks about his own family in today's Bible reading.

As their appearances are fleeting in the Gospels after the birth narratives, we tend to forget about Jesus' family (except for his mother, of course). Yet here they are, come to rescue him from his delusional state, and once again Jesus' response is probably not what we would consider appropriate. Shouldn't the Son of God be a bit more—well, polite? Later, he makes other comments about families in a similar vein: 'Anyone who loves their father or mother more than me is not worthy of me; anyone who loves a son or daughter more than me is not worthy of me' (Matthew 10:37). In Luke we find something even fiercer: 'If anyone comes to me and does not hate father and mother, wife and children, brothers and sisters… such a person cannot be my disciple' (14:26).

This brings us back once again to the importance of reading the Bible as a whole, because Jesus is not only using exaggeration here for rhetorical effect, just as preachers and speakers do today, but his remarks are made in the context of the covenant law, which included the commandment to 'honour your father and your mother' (Exodus 20:12). He is not saying that families do not matter, that we should get away from home and forget our parents as soon as we can. What he is doing, though, is making the point—cheering to some, puzzling to others—that family ties are not everything. There may be times when, as his disciples, we are called to make choices that flatly contradict our family loyalties, going right against the belief system that is part of our family identity. If, as a result, we find ourselves isolated from parents, siblings, or even our spouse or children, for the sake of the gospel, we have the reassurance that we are still part of the family of our Father in heaven.

We might assume that, if we turn the pages of scripture, we will find plenty of clear and helpful teaching about how we should manage our home relationships. While the New Testament epistles do contain some relevant verses, it can come as a shock to realise just how dysfunctional a lot of biblical families were. Setting aside the succession of wicked rulers that later afflicted the kingdoms of Israel and Judah, we find that even the patriarchs were a sorry shower as far as modern ideas of family values are concerned. Although cited by God himself when he spoke to Moses ('I am the God of your father, the God of Abraham, the God of Isaac and the God of Jacob', Exodus 3:6), the family histories of Abraham, Isaac and Jacob are littered with horrifying episodes of jealousy, cruelty, deceit, disrespect, rivalry and even incest.

If God could still honour his commitment to such an emotionally messy bunch, there is surely hope for us, however chaotic our family situations. Whatever relationships have unravelled, no matter how catastrophic the breakdown, we are not excluded from God's loving care if we come to him humbly, asking for his help. As the prophet Isaiah wrote, 'Surely the arm of the Lord is not too short to save, nor his ear too dull to hear' (Isaiah 59:1). The only thing that could make a separation between us and the Lord's inexhaustible compassion is our determination not to acknowledge that we might have played any part in what has gone wrong, our belief that somehow we are completely and utterly beyond reproach.

If we are blessed with a loving and supportive family, we should be alert to God's call to open our home in some way, so that 'family' becomes inclusive rather than exclusive. While the 1970s 'extended household' experiments by some churches seemed to create as many problems as they solved, the impulse behind the initiative was a bold attempt to shape a radical lifestyle in the spirit of the early Church (see Acts 2: 44–45). I have recently come across a number of congregations in which some members give up a private celebration and hold an extended and inclusive party. Other households take a simpler approach and make a point of inviting a visitor to share their family meal. We may find such ideas too challenging to adopt personally—but at least let us dare to pray that God will show us how we can share our blessing with others.

## For reflection

*'I kneel before the Father, from whom every family in heaven and on earth derives its name' (Ephesians 3:14–15).*

*

## 12 December

# PUTTING ON A GOOD SHOW

Woe to you who long for the day of the Lord! Why do you long for the day of the Lord? That day will be darkness, not light. It will be as though a man fled from a lion only to meet a bear, as though he entered his house and rested his hand on the wall only to have a snake bite him. Will not the day of the Lord be darkness, not light—pitch-dark, without a ray of brightness? I hate, I despise your religious festivals; I cannot stand your assemblies. Even though you bring me burnt offerings and grain offerings, I will not accept them. Though you bring choice fellowship offerings, I will have no regard for them. Away with the noise of your songs! I will not listen to the music of your harps. But let justice roll on like a river, righteousness like a never-failing stream!

AMOS 5:18–24

Let's admit it—this comes across as one of those ranting, upsetting Bible passages that can put people right off the Old Testament. Yet again a prophet goes off the deep end, making God sound intemperate, even bullying. It sounds outrageous, inexcusable, to say that he actually hates 'religious festivals', that the people's offerings are unacceptable, apparently taking no account of the time or money they would have spent preparing them. If God is supposed to be loving, why such rage? Such sentiments could not have any relevance to our worship—could they?

As we continue to stroll through this choice neighbour-hood on our Advent pilgrimage, we reach a particularly pleasant location: the substantial church surrounded by per-fectly manicured lawns and clipped hedges. The late 20th-century architecture may not be to every pilgrim's taste (we hear some muttering behind us about 'the excrescences of modernity'); the services advertised on the colourful posters suggest a liturgical approach inclining to the 'happy clappy' (another mutter from the back row)—but the general air is of a place to which young families flock. Fortunately, here, as in many parts of the country, there is a choice of worship venue. Rising above the rooftops we glimpse a historic-looking spire, and rumour has it that the next-door congregation regularly hosts the cathedral choir B team for Evensong amid marble pillars and appropriate hush.

Even more than Easter and Pentecost—in most local churches, anyway—Christmas is the season of the full-on special service, when more visitors cross the threshold than at any other time of year. Depending on personal taste and the choice on offer, these visitors come for choirboys in starched ruffs or for dressed-down worship bands moving skilfully through a repertoire of favourite carols with added drums and bass. The congregation may get a brief seasonal homily from the vicar to go with their Nine Lessons and Carols, or an invitation to an Alpha course in their welcome pack of notice sheet, Bible and gift aid envelope (the songs are all projected on to a rather high screen in *this* church).

Some visitors will return in the new year, buoyed by the unexpected warmth of the welcome. Others, having ticked the mental box of 'carol service', are happy to put church attendance out of mind along with the rest of the Christmas paraphernalia until next December. If we are regular worshippers, we may well have views on this latter line of action; whether or not we approve will depend on the extent to which we are happy for church to have 'fuzzy edges' in terms of membership. What we are unlikely to doubt is whether God is happy with our own approach to worship—because we're the good guys, surely. We're the ones who provide the music, give the talks, lead the prayers and serve refreshments afterwards. And, when they notice, people tell us that we're doing a good job.

What is troubling about our reading from Amos—admittedly one of the more strident of the prophets—is that even if we view it through the lenses of poetic imagery and exaggeration for dramatic effect, the underlying message is stark and clear. God's words of stern rebuke are for those who do, in fact, 'long for the day of the Lord', who bring the full range of offerings, who are members of the harp worship ensemble. Like us, they are the good guys, yet what God says to them is, 'Don't assume that your priorities are my priorities. Don't forget that the fear of the Lord is the beginning of wisdom. You call for my coming; have you reflected fully on what that means?'

Our Advent and Christmas worship, especially our singing of carols, can feel as familiar and comfortable as a pair of favourite slippers. We sing happily 'O come, let us adore him' or 'The angel of the Lord came down and glory shone around' and the words evoke no more than a pleasant haze of Christmases past and Christmases yet to come (for what carol service would dare to omit the golden oldies?). To paraphrase the American writer Annie Dillard, however, we should be filled with a rightful awe at what we are invoking—the splendour of the almighty and ever-living Creator of the universe. As she points out, perhaps crash helmets would be appropriate headgear for church services, rather than any more stylish but insubstantial fashions.[4]

It is frighteningly easy to get into a fixed mindset, a well-worn groove of expectation, in our worship, even if we are part of a congregation that prides itself on being 'open to the Spirit'. Human nature being what it is, we are inclined to expect the expected, to anticipate the challenge before it reaches our hearts, whether it comes through the laying on of hands by the prayer ministry team or the elevation of the Host by the priest, in a cloud of incense. The words of Amos the prophet should jerk us out of our comfort zone. We need to think about what kind of worship might be acceptable to God, and then ask him and be ready to receive his answer, rather than simply going along with what suits our personal tastes.

The conclusion of our passage makes clear the essential ingredients of acceptable worship from God's perspective. The prophet calls for torrents of 'justice' and 'righteousness' to flow. We have a God who cares for every one of his creatures, and the biblical witness is clear that if there is one group whom he specially favours, it is not the privileged but the poor. It will be clear time and again in the course of these Advent readings that social concern and action are not optional extras, the speciality of those who have an interest in such matters, but an integral part of the gospel message for the whole Church.

## For reflection

'Suppose a brother or sister is without clothes and daily food. If one of you says to them, "Go in peace; keep warm and well fed," but does nothing about their physical needs, what good is it? In the same way, faith by itself, if it is not accompanied by action, is dead' (James 2:15–17).

*

## 13 December

# BEING GREAT MEN AND WOMEN OF GOD

One of the teachers of the law ... asked [Jesus], 'Of all the commandments, which is the most important?' 'The most important one,' answered Jesus, 'is this: "Hear, O Israel: the Lord our God, the Lord is one. Love the Lord your God with all your heart and with all your soul and with all your mind and with all your strength." The second is this: "Love your neighbour as yourself." There is no commandment greater than these.' 'Well said, teacher,' the man replied. 'You are right in saying that God is one and there is no other but him. To love him with all your heart, with all your understanding and with all your strength, and to love your neighbour as yourself is more important than all burnt offerings and sacrifices.' When Jesus saw that he had answered wisely, he said to him, 'You are not far from the kingdom of God.'

MARK 12:28–34 (ABRIDGED)

Next to the church is where we often find the minister's house. Do we call it a manse, a vicarage, a rectory—even a parsonage? Perhaps we belong to a church tradition that does not have full-time paid leadership. Frankly, it doesn't matter that much (although, over the centuries, people have literally gone to the stake over similar issues). However a church is structured, there will always be those who are placed on a pedestal by congregation members, for a variety of reasons. There will also be those who hoist themselves on to a pedestal, discreetly or otherwise. Whether pedestals are offered or taken, what matters most is the spiritual health of the worshipping community, leaders and led alike.

The combination of authority and spirituality can be both potent and potentially toxic. In whatever church tradition we stand, the leader so easily ends up being seen as the sole hotline to God, which can result in the distorted view that it is the leader—and not God—who is the source of blessing, the means of healing, the well of grace. When news breaks of a church leader falling into error or sin, fingers are pointed and heads shaken, both inside and outside a church. How often, though, do church members look at themselves and ask, 'What have we done? How did we let things get to this pass?' It is true that some leaders choose to manipulate vulnerable people to fulfil their own unmet needs; it is equally true that some churches can be as hostile to mental health as any messed-up family. When things go wrong, it is too tempting simply to blame those in charge and not reflect on the part played by a congregation or by individuals within a congregation.

We can find it easy to criticise leaders who end up straying sexually, for example, if we have never had to face the temptations they may face. A friend of mine spoke at a national church event and was amazed by the unqualified adulation of those who crowded round afterwards, wanting an opinion on any number of subjects. My friend found it immensely flattering but also a bit frightening to be trusted so much, by so many strangers. An unchecked hunger for recognition, combined with such total admiration, may eventually lead to common-sense reactions being switched off, and the benefit of too many doubts being given, forgetting the fact that leaders are humans, just like everyone. And, in a worst case scenario, some kind of horrible crisis can occur.

Jesus' words in today's passage are a rock, a stable foundation, on which we can build both our lives as congregations and (particularly if we are leaders) our sense of calling. The bottom line is this: what matters is loving God and loving our neighbours as ourselves—which also means that we need to care for ourselves, something that leaders can be prone to forget. Loving God with all our heart, all our understanding and all our strength, and loving our neighbour as ourselves, is actually more important than all the mission action plans, church festivals, reordering schemes, outreach events and so on. Yes, these are important—but not as important as love.

We may well be so familiar with these words that the profound truth they convey sounds trite, no more than what we expect the Bible to say—a bit like dismissing *Hamlet* for being full of quotes. The challenge is to own the truth for ourselves, to check our assumptions, our decisions and our plans against the command to love God and to love our neighbour. Do we act out of love or are we driven, quite possibly unawares, by emotional hunger, anger or long-suppressed hurt? Have we ever paused long enough to ask ourselves whether we know what 'love' really means in this most fundamental of contexts?

In terms of healthy church life, Paul's teaching in 1 Corinthians 12 about each person playing their part in 'the body of Christ' remains the best of possible metaphors: 'God has put the body together... If one part suffers, every part suffers with it; if one part is honoured, every part rejoices with it' (vv. 24, 26). Leaders and members alike, we are interdependent, different but equally indispensable to the functioning of the body. Contrary to the world's values (values from which, sadly, the Church is not immune), in God's eyes there is no distinction between celebrities and consumers, heroes and hero-worshippers. We are all forgiven sinners; we are all great men and women of God, and the Spirit is at work within each one of us, shaping us so that day by day we embody more of this truth in our lives. And, of course, 1 Corinthians 12 is followed by 1 Corinthians 13, the hymn about love, which is placed above every other gift of healing, prophecy, miracles or tongues.

If we have the daunting responsibility and privilege of leadership, let us never forget the importance of exercising our task with deep humility. We should never lose a sense of astonishment that God Almighty may actually choose to work through our ministry; likewise, we should take care to avoid the folly of thinking that anything good that results is to do with our own spiritual power and righteousness, as opposed simply to being open to the prompting of the Spirit. Unlike most other public arenas in our world, there should be no room for prima donnas in the arena of the church.

Those of us who are church members, equal members of the body of Christ, have the responsibility and privilege of caring for those who lead us. Among our tasks is to help our leaders maintain healthy and balanced lives, loving themselves and their families and staying rooted in our worshipping community, which (all being well) will have a good system of checks and balances to encourage right conduct of authority, as well as a mixture of encouraging and testing situations. At the same time, we should be mindful of the wonderful knowledge that God can and will work through us, even if we feel far from 'expert'. Our word, prayerfully offered, can be the means of transformation that another has longed for; our smile the means of unexpected healing.

## For reflection

'Serve one another humbly in love… If you keep on biting and devouring each other, watch out or you will be destroyed by each other' (Galatians 5:13, 15).

*

## 14 December

# WHEN IT ALL COMES CRASHING DOWN

As the deer pants for streams of water, so my soul pants for you, my God. My soul thirsts for God, for the living God... These things I remember as I pour out my soul: how I used to go to the house of God under the protection of the Mighty One with shouts of joy and praise among the festive throng. Why, my soul, are you downcast? Why so disturbed within me? Put your hope in God, for I will yet praise him, my Saviour and my God... By day the Lord directs his love, at night his song is with me—a prayer to the God of my life. I say to God my Rock, 'Why have you forgotten me? Why must I go about mourning, oppressed by the enemy?' My bones suffer mortal agony as my foes taunt me, saying to me all day long, 'Where is your God?' ... Put your hope in God, for I will yet praise him, my Saviour and my God.
PSALM 42:1–5, 8–11 (ABRIDGED)

Our week in this pleasant part of the city has come to an end, but as we walk on we notice a sudden chill in the air. Here is a little parade of shops, but half are standing empty, bailiffs' orders posted on the doors, unclaimed mail strewn across the dusty floors. Here is an attractive house conversion (as estate agents would say), but both flats are fastened with steel shutters, having been repossessed by the mortgage company. Is this the trail left by those who borrowed recklessly, speculating in the hope of accumulating—or by those who were prudent, cautious but forced to overextend their finances simply to maintain a livelihood or afford a roof over their heads? An unexpected redundancy, a relationship breakdown or a much smaller but still significant change in circumstances means that, quite suddenly, almost everything that matters is lost.

The heading for this week's readings—'Earn all you can, save all you can, give all you can'—is the good advice originally offered by John Wesley, the itinerant evangelist and preacher whose ministry gave rise to the Methodist Church. It offers wise guidelines for living, an exhortation to be both hardworking and prudent and, at the same time, generous. Living by such a precept is, however, absolutely no guarantee that bad things will not happen to us. Yes, some people fall into what the biblical writers call folly, and end up paying a bitter price. Some are brought low through the actions of those they trusted. Some find their lives wrecked by ill health—their own or that of those for whom they care.

When life comes crashing down around our ears, it may not be much comfort to know that the ruins are the consequence of somebody else's behaviour rather than our own. The desolation looks and feels the same. Of course, our experience may not be a sudden catastrophe but a process of slow decay: we wake one morning and finally notice that our life is littered with atrophied hopes and shattered promises. At the end of our first week of readings, we reflected on how all things, both good and bad, come to an end—an inescapable fact of our mortality. Here we face the fact that however much we live by the rules, however careful we are, we cannot control every eventuality. Even if we try our utmost, we cannot order events to keep ourselves and those we love in perpetual health, happiness and safety.

Like so many of the psalms, our reading for today see-saws between hope and despair, rage at the injustice and disappointment of life and rejoicing in God's everlasting love. Such emotional volatility truly reflects how we feel when disaster strikes. We try to cling to what we know of God's goodness, while boiling with fear and anger that *this* should happen to *us*. For our worship to be heartfelt, we must make sure it has room to encompass dark feelings as well as bright, the Good Friday moments as well as Pentecost. If that is not the case, we can end up feeling exiled from our faith at the very time when we most need it to bridge the chasm that has opened up in our circumstances, as a result of whatever collapse we are enduring.

It is troubling, then, to reflect that while the psalms are an enduringly popular inspiration for hymns and worship songs, the songwriters tend to extract the hope and rejoicing and leave out the despair and disappointment.

We may be familiar with a musical setting of Psalm 42 that sweeps us along in a lyrical haze, as we imagine a kind of Bambi skipping through leafy glades and pausing for a refreshing sip from a babbling stream. What we need to bear in mind is the arid, Middle Eastern setting of much of scripture, which underlies the poetic imagery in this passage. This is not the New Forest or some other tranquil sylvan setting; the deer is desperate, dehydrated, panting for a life-giving drink, just as the soul of the psalmist is parched, having had nothing to quench thirst except salt tears. He seeks God in grim desperation; this search is a question of life or death, of enduring 'mortal agony', not simply a pleasant option to fill a Sunday morning.

In *Divorce—a Challenge to the Church*, a powerful and profound reflection on marriage breakdown, Bob Mayo uses the metaphor of exile to convey something of the associated disconnection and devastation. As the people of Israel, exiled to Babylon, had to learn to 'sing the Lord's song in a strange land' (Psalm 137:4, KJV), so those who have been divorced have to live through a wilderness season, and may find themselves searching for healing and recovery while still feeling far from home. Despite the profound sorrow of such exile, the possibility exists of eventual homecoming, even though there is no possibility of going back to 'before'. As Mayo writes, his reflections have a wider application:

*The idea of exile can be used as a metaphor… for Christian living more generally, and can be understood positively as well as negatively. Exile is a hopeful image of growth and potential as well as a negative image involving ideas of distance, alienation and separation, being away from home, excluded and unable to return.*[5]

The psalmists remind us again and again that no matter how calamitous our misfortunes, we can still cling to God's faithfulness and ask him to guide us back to a place of security and peace. As we walk the hard path that opens before us, we can call on him not only to deepen our understanding of who he is but also to give us the strength and courage to go on.

Let's remember, once again, that Advent is a season for looking forward, a time for reflecting on God's promises, for hope. Even if the place where we find ourselves right now is a bleak and dispiriting place of exile, even if we fear there is no safe road ahead and we will never return to anywhere that feels like home, we can take a deep breath and tell ourselves, as does our psalmist, 'Put your hope in God, for I will yet praise him, my Saviour and my God.'

## Prayer

*Lord, we long for your living water; come to us and quench our thirst, for without you we can go no further. Amen*

# *Heavenly perspectives*

After two weeks in the city, our pilgrimage now takes us beyond the suburbs, leaving the last few straggling houses behind, and up to a place where we can gain a wider perspective. Beyond this city there is a hill. You could call it a small mountain—anyway, it is steep enough to make us short of breath as we climb, and high enough for the summit to give us a view over the entire town and surrounding countryside. Here we will linger for the next seven days, for this is a place where we can reflect on the character of the God we worship. In fact, some argue that *El Shaddai*, one of God's Hebrew titles usually translated as 'God Almighty', can actually mean 'God of the mountain'.

Although I have lived mostly in relatively low-lying landscapes, I love mountains. For me, as for many others, reaching the summit and surveying the panorama opened below is about more than simply 'getting to the top'. It is about finding a new vantage point on the surrounding landscape—hence the disappointment of getting up there, only to discover that the view is blanketed in cloud.

As is clear from many biblical episodes, God is often encountered on mountain tops (and I guess this can include small mountains, not to say hills, too). Abraham was saved by divine intervention from sacrificing his only son on Mount Moriah (Genesis 22:1–19); Moses stayed 'forty days and forty nights' in the cloud of God's presence on Sinai (Exodus 24:18); Elijah heard the word of the Lord on Horeb (1 Kings 19:8–18); Jesus was transfigured by heavenly power on a mountain traditionally identified as Mount Tabor in Israel, appearing in glory with Moses and Elijah (Mark 9:2–8); the disciples were sent out with the good news from a final mountain-top meeting with Jesus (Matthew 28:16–20). Why should this be the case? Perhaps it is something to do with drawing apart from the everyday world, moving beyond the zone of normal human activity, to a place where there are fewer distractions from the task of focusing on God and what he might have to say to us.

This week we may not have the opportunity to climb a real-life mountain, but we can still ask God to grant us a new perspective on who he is and what he requires of us— a change in vantage point that can begin to shape and direct our hearts as we draw closer to Christmas itself.

*

*15 December*

# KNOWING OUR PLACE

Then the Lord spoke to Job out of the storm. He said: 'Who is this that obscures my plans with words without knowledge? Prepare to defend yourself; I will question you, and you shall answer me. Where were you when I laid the earth's foundation? Tell me, if you understand. Who marked off its dimensions? Surely you know! Who stretched a measuring line across it? On what were its footings set, or who laid its cornerstone—while the morning stars sang together and all the angels shouted for joy? ... What is the way to the abode of light? And where does darkness reside? Can you take them to their places? Do you know the paths to their dwellings? Surely you know, for you were already born! You have lived so many years!'
JOB 38:1–7, 19–21

On our modest mountain top, it is obvious that we are no longer in a setting exclusively shaped by human activity, although some of us have managed to squeeze on to the 'In loving memory' bench that somebody has managed to install here. Even if we look out on an expanse of neat fields rather than a tangle of primeval forest, however, we should think about the fact that the rock beneath our feet—whether visible or hidden by soil—is ancient beyond comprehension. We may carelessly kick aside a small stone, oblivious to the huge physical forces that shaped it and brought it to that place. A while ago, I read a picture book with my younger son, *The*

*Pebble in my Pocket*, which neatly conveyed the vastness of geological time in the story of a simple brown pebble that originates in a volcano 480 million years ago and is eventually picked up by a young girl in the present day.

If we are very familiar with the contours of a particular range of hills or mountains, either because we live nearby or because we have holidayed in the area, it is laughably easy to take them for granted as a decorative backdrop to daily life and forget that they were there eons before us and will endure (assuming no asteroid strikes) long after our very bones have turned to dust. Many visitors to the Hebrides go to marvel at the Lewisian Gneiss, a metamorphic rock formed more than 3000 million years ago—the oldest exposed rock in the world and half as old as the planet itself.

From time to time, people have written and spoken of an unexpected raw fear at realising the enormous scale, in terms of both size and longevity, of a mountainous landscape. They feel reduced, shrivelled into insignificance, in a way that is unlikely to happen in the consoling context of houses and streets. In *The Wild Places*, Robert MacFarlane describes a crushing sense of solitude and discomfort on the remote Scottish mountain where he spent the night: 'This place was not hostile to my presence, far from it. Just entirely, gradelessly indifferent… All travellers to wild places will have felt some version of this, a brief blazing perception of the world's disinterest. In small measures it exhilarates. But in full form it annihilates.'[6]

When confronted with such a diminishing of our own scale, the temptation for many of us is to fight back and assert our God-given dominion over the created world (see older translations of Genesis 1:28). We may not go so far as to build a road up a mountain (as, I gather, my great-grandfather did in Kenya) but we want confirmation that we matter, that we will not be forgotten, that our human bones are actually of more value than the bones of our planet. We do not, however, glean much comfort from a Bible passage such as today's, which comes from the concluding chapters of the book of Job.

We are so used to preachers telling us that we are made in the image of God, as the pinnacle of creation, that we sometimes forget how, according to the first chapter of Genesis, our planet—and our solar system, galaxy, universe—were also made for the Creator's delight, not merely as a stage set for humanity's appearance. The kind of mocking, rhetorical questions that God asks of Job (and it is well worth reading chapters 38—41 in full) are similar to the conundrums with which scientists continue to wrestle now. The sum of human knowledge is far greater today than at any other time in recorded history, yet both on the scale of the infinitely large and the infinitesimally small, there is still so much that even the most expert of experts do not understand. We may know a great deal—we may hold a university post in Earth Science, Astrophysics or Inorganic Chemistry—but we also need to know our place in relation to the Supreme Being.

Of course, there are also many Bible passages that tell us of our authority over creation. In Psalm 8, we read how we are made just 'a little lower than the heavenly beings', and that we are crowned with 'glory and honour' (v.5). We rule over 'all flocks and herds, and the animals of the wild, the birds in the sky, and the fish in the sea' (vv. 7–8). Astonishingly, given our puny size and unimpressive lifespan, God has decreed that it is up to us to care for the works of his hands. Right back in Eden, man was made the gardener. Paradise needed somebody to 'work it and take care of it' (Genesis 2:15); after the Fall, this task was not taken away from humanity but it did become much harder. I think it is safe to say, the general conclusion is that we have not carried out our task well.

I remember being at a Christian conference in the late 1980s when a speaker questioned whether we needed to care for the earth because 'it was all going to burn up anyway'. Thankfully, even the Church has moved on over the last couple of decades, and today many Christians are fully committed to issues of sustainable living and environmental conservation. The fact remains, however, that the human being is easily the most dangerous creature on the planet (that's a useful fact for impressing small children, by the way). Our challenge is to combine awareness of our terrible capacity to destroy with an awareness of God's original mandate to us— and also never to take for granted the immense age, dignity and beauty of our world, so much of which will outlast us.

On one of the long winter evenings this week, try to find your way to a place where you can see something of the night sky, as little obscured by streetlight as possible. Take time for your eyes to get used to the darkness and stare up at the stars (even better, use a pair of binoculars). If you can, find the Milky Way, watch for the rising of Orion, let the constellations compel your gaze, and feel your own importance diminish into a rightful sense of humility—and astonishment that the Creator of all that remote glory should care about us.

## Prayer

*Lord God, enlarge our vision to grasp more of the majesty of the world you have made for us—and help our hearts to overflow in thanks for the lavishness of your gift.*

*

## 16 December

# IMMANUEL—GOD WITH US

Jesus [said], 'I am the way and the truth and the life. No one comes to the Father except through me. If you really know me, you will know my Father as well. From now on, you do know him and have seen him.' Philip said, 'Lord, show us the Father and that will be enough for us.' Jesus answered: 'Don't you know me, Philip, even after I have been among you such a long time? Anyone who has seen me has seen the Father. How can you say, "Show us the Father"? Don't you believe that I am in the Father, and that the Father is in me? The words I say to you I do not speak on my own authority. Rather, it is the Father, living in me, who is doing his work. Believe me when I say that I am in the Father and the Father is in me; or at least believe on the evidence of the works themselves.'

JOHN 14:6–11

Christmas is the pre-eminent time in the Church's year when we think of the immanence as well as the transcendence of God. With the Gospel writer Matthew, we look back to Isaiah's prophecy of the virgin who gives birth to a son, 'Immanuel' (Isaiah 7:14), or 'God with us'. The Almighty, *El Shaddai*, remains above, beyond, surpassing us in every way; Immanuel, God with us, was actually formed in the body of a young woman, as close as it is possible for two separate beings to coexist. It would be easy, however, to fall into the error of thinking that until the coming of Jesus, God was remote from his creatures, the stereotypical 'angry Jehovah' that some readers of BRF's *New Daylight* notes occasionally cite when complaining about some of the more challenging Bible passages in their daily reading.

Our God has never been content to stay seated in glory on a heavenly throne, sending down occasional directives via his intermediaries. At the very beginning, in the story of Eden, we read of him 'walking in the garden in the cool of the day' (Genesis 3:8) as the man and his wife hid in shame. Whether or not we personally believe that this story is literally true or a more figurative account of a spiritual truth, the fact remains that whoever shaped the original narrative knew it was important to convey the reality of 'God with us', as close as someone strolling with companions in the warm dusk, just as friends still stroll together and enjoy the night breezes of summertime.

There are other places in the Old Testament where people have unexpected and tantalising encounters with 'God with us', when the realisation eventually dawns that there is more to the mysterious stranger (or strangers) than they first thought. The legendary film director Alfred Hitchcock had a habit of making cameo appearances in his films, catching the camera's eye in passing as the main action unfolded elsewhere. Our God does not limit himself to cameo roles, though; again and again he steps centre-stage to move things along, to stir people into action. When Abraham extends traditional Middle Eastern hospitality to three passing strangers (Genesis 18), it is only after they have rested, eaten lunch and talked, that there is any hint that here is 'the Lord' himself (v. 10), come to remind Abraham of the son promised as part of the covenant.

Jacob, maverick grandson of Abraham, wrestles with an

initially unidentified stranger on the night before a dreaded reunion with his estranged brother Esau. This 'God with us' experience is so physically demanding that Jacob is left with a permanent hip injury, as well as a blessing and a new name—Israel—and the knowledge that, as he states, 'I saw God face to face, and yet my life was spared' (Genesis 32:30). Later, in the book of Judges, Gideon is called to lead the Israelites against their marauding enemy by 'the angel of God', who is then revealed as the 'Sovereign Lord' himself, leading Gideon to cry out in fear that he will die after this face-to-face meeting (see Judges 6:11–24).

Gideon's fear was not without foundation; throughout scripture we are reminded that nobody can look on the face of God and live. The human body and mind can exist safely only within certain boundaries, both physical and mental; we are finite beings, designed for existence on a finite planet, although we bear in some way the image of God. He has, so the Teacher in Ecclesiastes tells us, 'set eternity in the human heart; yet no one can fathom what God has done from beginning to end' (3:11). Our Maker longs to draw close, to draw us closer to himself, but he can do so only if clothed in mortal flesh. In the coming of Jesus, the truth of Immanuel is presented in its most enduring and undeniable form.

In our passage today, Jesus spells out to his disciples that he is 'God with us', no longer a passing stranger but a young man who has been raised as part of a close-knit community, whose 'otherness' comes as a shock to all who think they know him, so that (as we read on 11 December) his own family assume he has gone mad (Mark 3:21). Do we detect a hint of exasperation in his words, 'Don't you know me, Philip, even after I have been among you such a long time?' For three years, the Son of God walks, talks, sleeps, eats, laughs, cries, loves. The divine power within him is such that his voice can raise the dead, and a faith-filled tug at his robe can heal. How can his companions not understand what is really going on?

We may pity those poor struggling fishermen, without pausing to reflect whether we truly understand who Jesus is. Our temptation is twofold: on the one hand, we forget that Jesus was fully human as well as fully God, and speak of him as a superhero whose sandals never touched the dusty Palestinian ground. It is easy to imagine that he just materialised in one place after another, dispensing God-magic en route to his appointment with destiny. On the other hand, we diminish him to a scale with which we can cope. Jesus becomes our best mate, always loving and affirming, somehow always coming to the same conclusions that we do. Yet here we are reminded of the jaw-dropping truth: 'Anyone who has seen me has seen the Father.' This fully human person is at the same time Immanuel, and his friends can see him, face to face.

What does the immanence of God mean for us right now, as we read this book, as we loiter on our mental mountain top, reflecting on the ways of the Creator? It does not mean that we can rest our physical gaze directly on the face of God; neither does it mean that we can glibly claim direct divine command for whatever we happen to feel like doing ('So I said to the Lord... and he said to me... so I say to you that we ought to...').

What we do have is the promise of Jesus made first to his disciples at the Passover meal, on the night before he died: 'I am in my Father, and you are in me, and I am in you' (John 14:20). Through the redemption effected by his sacrificial death, the way is open for us to be immersed in the Father's presence, and his Spirit infuses our hearts, breathing life into us and through us to bring healing and transformation to the world.

## Prayer

*Almighty God, open our eyes to see where and how you are present in our lives today.*

*

## 17 December

# THE WISDOM OF GOD

Does not wisdom call out? Does not understanding raise her voice? At the highest point along the way, where the paths meet, she takes her stand; beside the gate leading into the city, at the entrance, she cries aloud: 'To you, O my people, I call out; I raise my voice to all humanity. You who are simple, gain prudence; you who are foolish, set your hearts on it. Listen, for I have trustworthy things to say; I open my lips to speak what is right... By me kings reign and rulers issue decrees that are just; by me princes govern, and nobles—all who rule on earth. I love those who love me, and those who seek me find me. With me are riches and honour, enduring wealth and prosperity. My fruit is better than fine gold, what I yield surpasses choice silver. I walk in the way of righteousness, along the paths of justice, bestowing a rich inheritance on those who love me and making their treasuries full.
PROVERBS 8:1–6, 15–21

If you walk in the mountains, you need to be wise in the ways of maps and the dangers of exposure. Not long ago, I was reminded of how easy it is to be caught out, when thick mist descended just as I'd reached a mountain top with a family party ranging in age from 7 to 70. Thankfully, the descent route was fairly obvious but still treacherous in the early stages as we had to clamber over huge boulders slick with moisture. Wisdom comprises, to a significant extent, the recalling of past experiences, both as a guide to future action and as a warning to avoid past mistakes. Forgetting what is important can lead us along a steep and slippery descent into folly, not least the error of thinking that God's work in the world is entirely dependent on our own effortful initiatives.

Reflecting just a little about the history of Christianity in the British Isles, for example, reminds us that God's Spirit operates through every means possible, an unstoppable flood of living water spreading to the ends of the earth. At the beginning of the fifth century, a Romano-British teenager was kidnapped by what we would now call people-traffickers, and was sold into slavery in Ireland for six years. This devastating experience led him to discover for himself his family's Christian faith. Escaping from captivity, he nevertheless eventually returned to Ireland as a missionary, where he established a church that not only spread the gospel across that country but led to missionaries going out across Western Europe. We know him as St Patrick, patron saint of Ireland and mighty man of God.

Throughout scripture, God's people are called to remember what he has done for them in the past and what he promises to do for them in the time to come—provided they keep their part of the covenant relationship. The very fact that he constantly describes himself as 'the God of Abraham, Isaac and Jacob' is a reminder that he has remained faithful over generations; at the same time, his mysterious Name, as first revealed to Moses (Exodus 3:14), is 'I AM WHO I AM', an eternally present and existent Being. As he has been, so he is and will be. And today we come to consider a central attribute of God's character, which he longs to grow in us, his children—wisdom.

Just as we remembered St Nicholas on his 6 December feast day, so now we come to another ancient feature of the

Advent season, the first day of the 'O Antiphons'. These liturgical responses, originally in Latin, are addressed to Jesus Christ, each prefaced by 'O' and drawn primarily from the book of Isaiah. I was first introduced to the O Antiphons by the Revd Dr Gordon Huelin, venerable archivist at SPCK, where I worked for three years. He celebrated a weekly Eucharist in the small chapel at the SPCK offices, and, in the weeks before Christmas, he spoke of *Sapientia* (Wisdom), followed by *Adonai* (Lord), *Radix Jesse* (the Root of Jesse), *Clavis David* (Key of David), *Oriens* (Morning Star), *Rex Gentium* (King of the Nations), and lastly Immanuel.

The first antiphon, addressed to Jesus as the Wisdom of God, is inspired in part by Isaiah 11:2–3: 'The Spirit of the Lord will rest on him—the Spirit of wisdom and of understanding, the Spirit of counsel and of might, the Spirit of the knowledge and fear of the Lord—and he will delight in the fear of the Lord'. Our passage for today, from Proverbs 8, is often cited as a foretelling of Christ himself, as Wisdom (personified here as female) is described as the first of God's works, formed 'long ages ago, at the very beginning, when the world came to be' (see vv. 22–23).

Wisdom stands at the crossroads, near the gate that everybody has to pass to enter the city, and she yells out her offer like a market trader. Compared with the wealth generated by human commerce, what she offers is 'better than fine gold... [or] choice silver' (v. 19), a 'rich inheritance' (v. 21). In this poetic scene, all the people, including the 'simple' and 'foolish', have a chance to hear her. It is up to them whether they linger to hear more or walk away, risking the harm that she warns them against (v. 36).

What exactly are the qualities of this Wisdom? In Proverbs 9, we find a succinct—and famously misunderstood—

definition: 'The fear of the Lord is the beginning of wisdom, and knowledge of the Holy One is understanding' (v. 10). There is an understandable tendency to read 'fear' in the modern sense of 'fearful' rather than the older sense of 'deep respect', which causes some to wonder why God might possibly want us to be afraid of him. What is more, in today's culture where self-respect, personal space and autonomy are unquestioned priorities, the very idea of 'deep respect' can seem passé, especially when it involves a respectful attitude towards somebody else's person and possessions, rather than aggressive defence of ourselves and possibly the other members of our social or family 'tribe'.

In fact, the more we come to know of God—who he is, what he has done, what he promises to do—the more we come to appreciate the reverence and honour due to him. Even the most self-respecting, not to say self-regarding, 21st-century individual will accord honour to those who personify most thoroughly the values that that individual holds most dear, whether they be sporting prowess, business acumen or skateboarding skill. When we begin to be transformed by the Spirit's presence within us, our lives start to exhibit the characteristics of God's family; our values become our Father's values. As Jesus himself delighted in the 'fear of the Lord' and was filled with all the characteristics of the Spirit that Isaiah 11 describes, we as his brothers and sisters will find ourselves learning to delight in loving, honouring and, in a right sense, fearing our infinite Father, as we start to glimpse something of the expanses of his grace and generosity.

## For reflection

'The person without the Spirit does not accept the things that come from the Spirit of God but considers them foolishness, and cannot understand them because they are discerned only through the Spirit' (1 Corinthians 2:14).

*

*18 December*

# THE KINDNESS OF GOD

The Lord is my shepherd, I lack nothing. He makes me lie down in green pastures, he leads me beside quiet waters, he refreshes my soul. He guides me along the right paths for his name's sake. Even though I walk through the darkest valley, I will fear no evil, for you are with me; your rod and your staff, they comfort me. You prepare a table before me in the presence of my enemies. You anoint my head with oil; my cup overflows. Surely your goodness and love will follow me all the days of my life, and I will dwell in the house of the Lord for ever.
PSALM 23

Whether hillwalking in a rainy bit of Britain or on pilgrimage in a desert landscape, journeying with a group will go more smoothly if we have a good leader. Now, as you have envisioned the Advent pilgrimage in this book, you may or may not have also imagined a leader. If you did, chances are that you imagined an individual incorporating such qualities as reliability, calmness, patience and kindness, as well as the all-important ability to make decisions. In addition, this individual would probably be prepared to spend plenty of time with the walkers who needed a bit more assistance, rather than focusing on those easily able to maintain the pace of the expedition.

Being left behind, in whatever context, is hurtful. Even if no verbal judgment is passed, our slowness or weakness will be humiliatingly apparent as the main party forges ahead while we struggle along at the back. Somebody I know well still remembers, many years later, a fortnight at an adventure camp where the hillwalking activity turned out to be a long-drawn-out torture. Although a relatively active teenager, she found herself time and again literally crawling up a slope to join the rest of the team, who would wait until she reached their feet before striding off on legs of steel for the next peak. When, as an adult, she discovered that a truism of mountain safety is that the pace should be set by the slowest, it dawned on her for the first time that perhaps her jolly group leader had been less than professional in his approach.

The trouble is that too many of us are likely to blame ourselves for not keeping up, rather than questioning a dominant ethos of 'faster, stronger, quicker'. Whether in an exercise class, at academic study or even in a church service, we may mentally harangue ourselves for failing to maintain appropriate speed, when in fact our response is a perfectly natural one. If we never find a leader/teacher who tells us that, yes, they understand our response and, yes, they will help us find a way to keep going and eventually catch up, we may abandon our attempt altogether. An alternative outcome is equally sad: through sheer desperation, we finally make it to the front but then in turn begin to scorn the weak and vulnerable, fearing to end up again as they are. In effect, we are on the way to becoming bullies.

As we have thought about the character of God this week, we have been humbled before his majesty, awed at his wisdom and swept away by his graciousness in coming among us. Now it is time to reflect on the kindness of God. Today's reading, the best-loved of the psalms, is perhaps so familiar that we cease to absorb the healing impact of the picture story it creates. It is true that our God is Lord of space and time, the Master of the universe, but scripture tells us here (and elsewhere) that he is also like an old-fashioned shepherd, ambling at the pace of grazing animals, not actually doing a great deal most of the time except keeping watch, making sure that no harm comes to those in his care.

Our Pastor (the Latin for 'shepherd', as we may once have been told but have quite likely forgotten) waits patiently for his sheep until they have eaten and drunk enough to sustain them on the journey. He ensures that they do not stray too far from his presence, and he is a supremely protective presence when danger threatens. This image of God as kindly Shepherd reaches its most complete expression in Jesus, who told his followers, 'I am the good shepherd; I know my sheep and my sheep know me—just as the Father knows me and I know the Father—and I lay down my life for the sheep' (John 10:14–15). Not only does the Shepherd care for his sheep; he is willing to die in order to rescue them.

A while ago, I attended a Quiet Day where a fellow participant shared a question that had challenged her: whether or not she believed that God is good. Being raised in a Christian home, she knew that the answer was supposed to be an emphatic 'yes'. Over time, though, she had come to realise that knowing the right answer is not the same as believing it. She eventually gained the courage to acknowledge to herself that she found it quite hard to believe that God is good. Rather than being an obstacle to faith, this admission proved to be a step on the road to discovering for the first time something of his true and eternal goodness.

We may be confident that God is good, but do we believe that the one we worship is truly kind? The root meaning of the adjective 'kind' is linked to words such as 'kinship' and 'kindred', meaning those to whom we are linked by family ties. In other words, kindness is what we show to our kin. If we know ourselves to be part of God's family, we should be able to trust that he is indeed kind, because he is our Father. Sadly, for a significant number of people, 'kindness' is not a word easily associated with 'family'. Calling God Father, in particular, has become a sticking point for many, who feel they can only associate the title with a relationship marked by emotional distance and disapproval, even abuse.

That God is a good Shepherd, a kind Leader and a loving Father is revealed in this: he comes to us in a way that takes account of who we are and what we can comprehend. It is tempting to think that we can readily define his ways of working, that certain forms of music or words or gestures are the best way to guarantee a divine encounter for everybody, when in fact we have simply discovered a way that particularly suits our personality. Some will experience intimacy with the Father through exuberant band-led worship, some through solitary prayer in a place of profound quiet. Some will find the healing they seek in a dramatic anointing in full gaze of the congregation, others in something as simple as a loving embrace.

If we have experienced little by way of kindness in our own lives (although we may be very familiar with discipline and efficiency), we may need to make a point of asking God to develop this particular attribute within us. If we have the courage to admit that, yes, there is more than a touch of the bully about us, we can humbly confess our cruelty and ask for a work of God's grace and mercy in our lives. If we simply find that we cannot believe in the kindness of God, let us ask him to reveal himself to us—and then wait to see what happens.

## For reflection

*Would visitors to our local church get a sense of God's kindness from what they experience—or do we tend to emphasise either his power or his mystery?*

*

## 19 December

# OBEDIENCE

As Jesus started on his way, a man ran up to him and fell on his knees before him. 'Good teacher,' he asked, 'what must I do to inherit eternal life?' ... Jesus looked at him and loved him. 'One thing you lack,' he said. 'Go, sell everything you have and give to the poor, and you will have treasure in heaven. Then come, follow me.' At this the man's face fell. He went away sad, because he had great wealth. Jesus looked round and said to his disciples, 'How hard it is for the rich to enter the kingdom of God!' ... Then Peter spoke up, 'We have left everything to follow you!' 'Truly I tell you,' Jesus replied, 'no one who has left home or brothers or sisters or mother or father or children or fields for me and the gospel will fail to receive a hundred times as much in this present age: homes, brothers, sisters, mothers, children and fields—along with persecutions—and in the age to come eternal life.'

MARK 10:17, 21–23, 28–30

In the introduction to this week's readings, I spoke of how often the Bible shows people encountering God on mountains. It is debatable whether God is more likely to speak to people when they are in some kind of special place (up a mountain, in a church, at a famous place of pilgrimage), or whether people seek out such places specifically to focus on the things of God. However it works—and the answer probably involves elements of both—if we feel that we have been blessed by experiencing the presence of God in a closer way, we face a question closely followed by a challenge. The question is: what does God require of us? The challenge is: will we be obedient to his call to the life that he has purposed for us, which may prove to be very different from what we anticipated?

This episode from Mark's Gospel brings to mind the verses from the prophet Micah, 'What does the Lord require of you? To act justly and to love mercy and to walk humbly with your God' (6:8). The working out in practice, in real-life decisions, of such principles is what confounded the man in our reading, whom, we are told, Jesus saw and loved. Jesus wasn't trying to catch him out with the breathtaking command to relinquish his entire fortune; he was extending an invitation to live boldly, to be ready to set aside everything in order to gain the treasures of the kingdom. As it turned out, the command asked more than the man was prepared to yield. Cushioned by the ease and security afforded by wealth, the risk of losing that ease and security seemed to him to outweigh the heavenly riches that Jesus offered.

The issue is not whether material wealth is good or bad in itself. The Bible teaches elsewhere that as long as we do not allow money to become our god or the love of our life (easier said than done), it is a blessing, albeit one with enormous responsibilities (as we reflected on 8 December). The issue here is how open we are to hearing the Lord's requirement for our lives, a requirement that will be different for each of us, depending on what constitutes our personal security blanket. The more we have, whether in terms of possessions, relationships or supportive local community, the harder the prospect of relinquishing it, if that is what God asks of us. Even if we ask for God's daily blessing on our lives, we probably do not expect a blessing that involves any kind of poverty, even though Jesus preached that the poor should be considered blessed, because the kingdom was theirs (Luke 6:20; note that they are described as the 'poor in spirit' in the equivalent passage in Matthew 5:3).

The trouble is, it is quite possible that God's call may require us to travel outside—perhaps far outside—our comfort zone. We could find a hard road opening before us, one that leads us away from our mental map and into a metaphorical wilderness, where any reminders of familiar environments and familiar faces become treasured memories. Our journey through life may mean days, months or years of travelling off the comfortable highway, bumping along untarred tracks through rocky landscapes—initially exciting but ultimately exhausting. Even if we know that Jesus told his followers that coming his way meant 'taking up their cross' (see Mark 8:34–35), being prepared to lose everything, including life itself, it is tempting to put this sentiment in the 'rabbinical exaggeration' category, so that we don't have to dwell for long on the implications for our own lives.

This is, however, what Jesus was prepared to do in obedience to his Father. In the three short years of his earthly work, he took a road that led not to public adulation as the greatest teacher of the law that Israel had ever seen, but to a death involving the fullest and most public shame by the standards of both Roman and Jewish cultures. It would surely have occurred to his mother Mary, at various points during those three years, that her eldest son's life was not turning out as she had expected. Setting aside the marvels of his conception and birth, what about that day in his boyhood when he sat in the temple courts and astounded the elders with his wisdom (Luke 2:47)? Perhaps, though, she also remembered how, even at the age of twelve, Jesus put obedience to his Father's wishes above all other considerations (v. 49).

One particularly insidious temptation that can beset those in any kind of church leadership, weakening their ability to respond in obedience to God's call, is the understandable desire for public recognition. In some ways, we can feel that we are being courageous in renouncing a degree of material prosperity and conventional social status to serve the church—but perhaps we still secretly nurture hopes of a prestigious job, or at least a situation where we can go boldly in and build up a worshipping community so large and thriving that it becomes prestigious in itself. The recent focus on profiling personal strengths, discovering our leadership 'type' and so on, can make it harder to accept that our personal calling is to a hidden work, not a centre-stage ministry. The blessing of poverty that God longs to give us sometimes involves poverty of status, too. Are we open to the idea of serving in the army of God as a second lieutenant known only to a few, not as a general with a chest-load of medals? While the history of Christian mission around the world highlights a select band of heroes, for example, there were many others whose long years of toil and sacrifices have been forgotten over the passage of time.

Obedience is costly; like the man in today's passage, we may want to walk away, turning our gaze from Jesus' loving challenge. As we hesitate, though, we should remember the (somewhat double-edged) promise that he makes to his friends in the final verses. Whatever we have to give up for the sake of the gospel, we will receive far more in return, and in this life, too. With such gifts will also come 'persecutions', it is true, but those in turn are balanced by the promise of life beyond life, a hope so transcendent that it will transport us into the 'age to come'.

## Prayer

*Jesus, our Lord and Brother, grant us courage to follow in your footsteps. Make us brave enough to submit to the Father's will, just as you did, even if it costs us everything.*

*

*20 December*

# THANKFULNESS

Praise the Lord, my soul; all my inmost being, praise his holy name. Praise the Lord, my soul, and forget not all his benefits—who forgives all your sins and heals all your diseases, who redeems your life from the pit and crowns you with love and compassion, who satisfies your desires with good things so that your youth is renewed like the eagle's. The Lord works righteousness and justice for all the oppressed. He made known his ways to Moses, his deeds to the people of Israel: the Lord is compassionate and gracious, slow to anger, abounding in love… From everlasting to everlasting the Lord's love is with those who fear him, and his righteousness with their children's children—with those who keep his covenant and remember to obey his precepts.

PSALM 103:1–8, 17–18

Before we leave our mountain top, let's look out for one last time at the scene spread before us in the low, yellow light of the short winter day. The light touches the cityscape with carnivalesque brightness; even the dingy tower blocks bordering the gentrified neighbourhoods turn the colour of old gold. Does the gaze of God work this way on the world, its radiance transfiguring whatever it rests upon, finding beauty and possibility where we are lazily inclined to see only shabbiness and decay?

When we turn our gaze on our lives, do we see the

goodness and wonder of what we have, or do we focus on the areas where we feel short-changed? A combination of national culture, upbringing and personal taste predisposes us to have particular preferences as to what constitutes 'good' or 'nice', which may (depending on how perfectionist we are) doom us to endless dissatisfaction because life is never quite 'good/nice enough'. A 'nice life' may involve a tastefully decorated house, an attractive set of children, a job that gives us status and self-respect, a second home or third car—or any one of the infinite variations possible in such matters. The approach of midlife can act as an unwelcome wake-up call, as we realise the extent to which our assumptions of such a 'nice life' have not been achieved.

If we dare to allow the Spirit of God to adjust our perception of ourselves, it can be a profoundly transformative moment. An inner monologue of dissatisfaction, complaint and demands for 'more', 'better' or just 'different' becomes instead a litany of thankfulness. As we survey the land from our mountain-top, so the psalmist in our reading (identified as King David himself) surveys everything that the Lord does for his people—'all his benefits'—and his heart overflows with praise. Take a moment to read the whole psalm and notice how it encompasses thanksgiving for personal blessing, for covenant faithfulness ('he made known his ways to Moses') and for a holy, eternal God who loves and cares for his microscopic creatures ('he remembers that we are dust'). It calls on the whole of creation, from heavenly beings to 'all his works everywhere in his dominion', to offer praise.

We are told that the Lord forgives, heals, satisfies and renews us. This is our God, and the more we know of him, the more we find we can trust him and so praise him with sincere hearts, because we can believe with confidence that his love is 'from everlasting to everlasting'. Bearing in mind yesterday's reflections on obedience, we should remember the wider context for that calling and its cost: we offer obedience not to an alarmingly capricious Zeus figure but to one whose fundamental character is summarised in scripture as 'compassionate and gracious, slow to anger, abounding in love' (v. 8; see also Exodus 34:6; Joel 2:13; Jonah 4:2; Psalm 86:15 and elsewhere). If we take a long and prayerful look at our circumstances, we will start to be able to trace God's good and generous hand at work, providing the things that we need when we need (and that is not the same as 'want') them.

At the same time, it can be a bit too easy to think in terms of thankfulness simply for what God has given us personally, although we may stretch our frame of reference to include our extended family or church community. Psalm 103 reminds us that we need to look at the bigger movements of history, searching and giving thanks for signs of God's provision for his children beyond the parameters of our own lifetimes, considering how he has worked through the tides and currents of human activity to bring about his purpose of 'reconciling the world to himself' (2 Corinthians 5:19). This is not to endorse the mindset that proclaims glibly, 'God is on our [winning] side', nor yet the idea that we are simply toys controlled by a celestial puppet master. Rather, it reminds us that this is God's world and we are part of a greater picture than we can imagine. As members of the human race, it is incumbent upon us to thank God for what he has done and is doing on a cosmic scale.

Thankfulness and obedience go hand in hand. If we find that ours is a hard calling, leading us into desert places, those experiences can change us for the better, teaching us gratitude for what we would otherwise take for granted. In a similar way, those who have known times of real hunger find it hard to assume thereafter that the food supply is permanently secure, and those who have endured serious illness or lost a supportive friendship recall with yearning the blessings that were previously an accepted part of normal life. And when our road leads us into easier places—as it surely will, even if it takes longer than we would like—we may find we have been gifted with enhanced attitudes of thankfulness and appreciation that we can (sensitively) share with others.

In *Embracing a Concrete Desert* (BRF, 2010), Lynne Chandler shares a powerful and personal account of experiencing wilderness times, and describes some of the hard but important lessons she learned about thankfulness as a result. Moving to Cairo for her husband's work, she struggled for emotional survival in the hot, dusty chaos of one of the world's biggest cities. Over time, however, she discovered that she could 'embrace the desert', finding peace and even joy in unlikely situations. She began to see the beauty of the city sunsets, even though they were caused by a stifling blanket of smog. Instead of endlessly grieving the loss of the green spaces of her old home, she began to delight in the shade of the single tree near their Egyptian apartment. On the banks of the Nile, she savoured the powerful symbolism of the life-giving river flowing through barren places.

We express our thanks to God for the gifts he gives us because that is the response of love. He knows the thoughts of our hearts before we express them, but to hear our thanks gives him an infinitely greater measure of the delight that a human parent feels when a tiny baby first learns to smile. The parental care is not dependent on the smile, but the smile marks the beginning of a true relationship, a giving and receiving of love that grows and deepens over a lifetime and, in the case of our relationship with God, in the eternity thereafter.

## For prayer

'Give us that due sense of all thy mercies, That our hearts may be unfeignèdly thankful, And that we show forth thy praise, Not only with our lips, but in our lives; By giving up ourselves to thy service, and by walking before thee in holiness and righteousness all our days.'

FROM THE GENERAL THANKSGIVING, BOOK OF COMMON PRAYER (1662)

*

## *21 December*

# EXPECTANCY

'At that time the kingdom of heaven will be like ten virgins who took their lamps and went out to meet the bridegroom. Five of them were foolish and five were wise. The foolish ones took their lamps but did not take any oil with them. The wise, however, took oil in jars along with their lamps. The bridegroom was a long time in coming, and they all became drowsy and fell asleep. At midnight the cry rang out: "Here's the bridegroom! Come out to meet him!" Then all the virgins woke up and trimmed their lamps. The foolish ones said to the wise, "Give us some of your oil; our lamps are going out." "No," they replied, "there may not be enough for both us and you. Instead, go to those who sell oil and buy some for yourselves." But while they were on their way to buy the oil, the bridegroom arrived. The virgins who were ready went in with him to the wedding banquet. And the door was shut. Later the others also came. "Sir! Sir!" they said, "Open the door for us!" But he replied, "Truly I tell you, I don't know you."'

MATTHEW 25:1–12

Note the date: it is Midwinter's Day, the shortest day (or the longest night) of the year in the northern hemisphere. Christmas is almost upon us. It is time to come down from the mountain top and retrace our path through the twilight back into the city, where preparations for the festivities are entering their final, frenzied phase.

We should be careful as we go down, because accidents are more likely to happen during a descent than on the way up. People begin to hurry, thinking that they are confident of the route, that the journey is nearly over, and a momentary stumble can turn into a disastrous fall, especially if the light is failing faster than expected. In a similar way, if we are ever tempted to think, 'Well, that's God sewn up, then', we should be mindful of the biblical injunction, 'Be careful that you don't fall!' (1 Corinthians 10:12). Yes, he is loving, faithful, forgiving, generous, infinite yet immanent; but today's reading reminds us that we must be ready for his coming among us and we cannot assume that it will be at a time and place of our convenience.

As at the close of the first and second weeks of our readings, the Bible passage here at the end of the third week sounds a disquieting note. This is not one of those parables of Jesus that pops up in children's picture books as frequently as the lost sheep (or son or coin). Some of us may still be singing the old 'Sing hosanna' chorus in church—'Give me oil in my lamp... keep me burning till the break of day'—without recalling the original story, which is considerably less upbeat in tone. The context is that the wedding could not start until the bridegroom's arrival, so the bridesmaids ('bridesmaids' and 'virgins' being synonymous at the time) should have been ready. Having said that, Jesus points out that the bridegroom was 'a long time in coming'—so long, in fact, that the wedding party had dozed off. We could speculate that the bride was in a less-than-tranquil frame of mind and the whole occasion was threatening to fall rather flat. Then, at midnight, finally, the cry goes up: 'He is coming!' The wise are prepared; the foolish are not. When they arrive late at the party, they are confronted with not only a shut door but a firm refusal. The hour came and has now passed.

The parable comes in a section of Matthew's Gospel that contains much teaching on 'signs of the end times', with an emphasis on the warning, 'Keep watch, because you do not know on what day your Lord will come' (24:42; see also 25:13). As we have already noted more than once, Advent is the season of the Church's year set aside for reflection on 'end times', the promised return of Christ at the end of history. It is a further development of the 'day of the Lord' theme that we considered last week, a cataclysmic event to be anticipated with awe rather than naive enthusiasm.

Expectancy is not to be confused with fearful anticipation or wild-eyed speculation, however. I recall, while growing up in the 1970s, some adults getting more than a little excited by Christian books such as Hal Lindsey's *The Late, Great Planet Earth* and rock musician Larry Norman's depressing lyrics about being 'left behind' (also the title of a recent bestselling series of novels by Tim LaHaye). The general idea was that Christians would be snatched away from Earth in an event known as the 'rapture' (proponents citing what was actually a misreading of 1 Thessalonians 4:15–17 to substantiate their belief), leaving unbelievers to drown or possibly fry on a doomed planet. This was a source of some anxiety for me. Parents late collecting me from school? House a bit too quiet after lights-out? Perhaps the rapture had happened and I had been Left Behind. Too bad I thought I was a Christian; it just went to show that I couldn't be sure I was really saved. While clinging to faith out of fear of damnation rather than in response to God's invitation of love is a kind of commitment, it is a poor, threadbare one, in danger of being jettisoned as life begins to offer more appealing securities. The 'Repent, for the end is nigh' school of evangelism, please take note!

Another less-than-desirable response to the prospect of Christ's return is the 'Why bother?' frame of mind, evidenced notably by the Christians in Thessalonica, back in the earliest years of the Church. The apostle Paul scolded them for declining to work for a living (2 Thessalonians 3:6–15), telling them categorically that as nobody knew the due date for the second coming, they couldn't count on it as a handy excuse for a short but sweet life of leisure. Better the attitude of the admittedly flippant T shirt/fridge magnet slogan: 'Jesus is coming—look busy'.

Nearly 2000 years have passed since Paul warned the Thessalonians, so we can assume that the Day is now closer than ever, but that is still no reason to disappear with a party of friends and relations into the backwoods with twelve months' supply of tinned food and an arsenal of shotguns, fleeing the coming days of tribulation. Neither should we use the imminence of Christ's return as an excuse for blowing our church's budget on grandiose and unsuitable ministries, confident that our Lord will arrive in time to winch us out of the resultant financial hole. Let's reflect again on the vastness of geological time—or at least the fact that there has still been so much more 'BC' than 'AD'. The pace of world events may seem to be speeding up, moving to some kind of climax, but there have been many false alarms over the centuries and we are called not to scaremongering but to watchfulness.

Jesus told the parable of the bridesmaids to teach his audience about the importance of expectancy, of being prepared. The wise bridesmaids fell asleep with the others, so long was their wait, but they had thought to plan ahead. They were as surprised as their foolish friends by the late hour of the groom's coming, but they had ensured that they were ready to play their rightful part in the wedding celebrations.

We should heed Jesus' call to 'watch and pray' (Matthew 26:41), knowing that we are living between times, between the first and second comings. While only the Father knows the hour (see Matthew 24:36), what is not in doubt is that he will come again, one day.

## *For reflection*

*Christ has died, Christ has risen, Christ will come again.*

# Pilgrims to the manger

We have spent two weeks in the city centre and suburbs, seeking to hear God's voice amid the seasonal noise and examining the values and motives of our own hearts. We have spent a week outside the city, trying to glimpse something of God's perspective on human affairs. Now our Advent journey has brought us back into the city. The thought of doing any kind of 'big picture' reflection in this hectic, list-making, box-ticking week may seem pointless. If we don't try to carve out some time for this, however, we may well find that when we finally come to Christmas itself, the day can turn hollow, collapsing in on itself because we have neglected its core meaning.

In search of somewhere to ponder the significance of the Christmas events, we are going to sojourn in a cathedral. Of course, 'God with us' means that we can worship anywhere and that we don't have to use conventionally designated 'sacred space' in order to pray. I know that some will find the very idea of cathedrals suspect (although to emulate the old Soviet authorities and turn them into swimming pools or granaries is perhaps a step too far…), but even in secularised Europe, cathedrals remind us of a different set of priorities. The cathedral of our pilgrimage is not the most ancient, beautiful or frequently visited; it was not the site of major historical events, although Cromwell's army may have shot the heads off some carved angels, and earlier reformers were enthusiastic with the whitewash. But it is the place where many from this city will gather to celebrate Immanuel in word and song, even if a number are unsure of the full personal implications of what they are celebrating.

We will also have some unexpected encounters this week because of the interplay of light and shadow that characterises the Church calendar. On the very day after the heart-warming glow of Christmas, we confront the full costliness of following Jesus; we will walk out of step with the obligatory Yuletide benevolence of our post-Christian culture and consider the way of the cross.

*

## 22 December

# PUTTING CHILDREN IN THEIR PLACE

[Jesus and his disciples] came to Capernaum. When he was in the house, he asked them, 'What were you arguing about on the road?' But they kept quiet because on the way they had argued about who was the greatest. Sitting down, Jesus called the Twelve and said, 'Anyone who wants to be first must be the very last, and the servant of all.' He took a little child whom he placed among them. Taking the child in his arms, he said to them, 'Whoever welcomes one of these little children in my name welcomes me; and whoever welcomes me does not welcome me but the one who sent me.' … People were bringing little children to Jesus for him to place his hands on them, but the disciples rebuked them. When Jesus saw this, he was indignant. He said to them, 'Let the little children come to me, and do not hinder them, for the kingdom of God belongs to such as these.' … And he took the children in his arms, placed his hands on them and blessed them.

MARK 9:33–37; 10:13–16 (ABRIDGED)

We enter our cathedral through the grand, nail-studded West Door, via the inevitable glassed-in lobby designed to conserve both heat and the sanity of the cathedral cleaners (it provides a shoe-wiping area). We emerge into a moderately magnificent nave—but instead of hearing ethereal organ music, or at least some prerecorded plainsong, we see ahead a shambolic crowd of dressing-gowned, tea-towelled infants. It is the dress rehearsal for the nativity play.

To curb any irritation at this spectacle, we should bear in mind the ancient (but only relatively recently revived) tradition of mystery plays, those high points of medieval life when citizens came together to re-enact the key points of the Christian story. Banned along with so much else at the Reformation, the enduring popularity of these events is evidenced by the crowds who flock these days to the Wintershall Nativity in Surrey (which has been described as 'England's Oberammergau'), as well as similar performances in Chester, Lincoln and Barnsley. In our cathedral cast, we see a rather smug-looking Mary, clutching an unconvincingly blonde-haired doll, and a horde of bovine, ovine and even porcine extras. Nevertheless, they are unknowing descendants of a fine spiritual heritage, whereby you enact a truth in order to absorb it more fully.

Moreover, as our Bible reading for today forcibly reminds us, we need to put children in their place in the context of God's kingdom—and, as Jesus himself pointed out, that place is at the very centre. He tells his audience that the kingdom belongs to them, unlike the rich, well-educated young man whom we encountered last week, or even the rabbi from the week before, who was at least judged to be 'not far from the kingdom'. Unfortunately, we find it almost impossible to consider this idea without lapsing into treacly sentiment, especially at this time of year. The little ones—God bless 'em! They remind us what it is all about, don't they?

We must remember that Near Eastern culture at the time did not sentimentalise children or childhood; such attitudes are a post-Enlightenment phenomenon of the (over)developed world, in which our offspring are indulged, idealised and cosseted. Children were small and unimportant, even more marginalised than women, of value only because they ensured another pair of hands to sustain the subsistence economy and a guarantee of comfortable old age for their parents. Their role was to mature and become a useful part of the community as soon as possible. So what do Jesus' words imply? What is it about children that gifts them with such importance in the eyes of the Son of God?

Children, then and now, have a tendency to view things with an embarrassing degree of clarity and directness. Often unaware of what they ought to see or say, they have not shut down the avenues of curiosity in the way that the rest of us have. Their questions and comments are likely to wrongfoot the best-prepared adult at times: 'Why? But why? Why is it really like that? What exactly do you mean? I don't understand —tell me all over again.' They have the mental space and innate inclination to worry away at questions that most of us are relieved to file away under the heading of 'pending—not for review until bereavement/redundancy/national disaster/ imminent death'. We would do well, during this week of Christmas reflections, to allow ourselves something of the childlike tendency to brood over the bits of faith that we don't understand, rather than letting it wash over us in a tidal wave of seasonal loveliness.

Another characteristic of children, both then and now, is that—as much as they can—they play. In recent years, much erudite ink has been spilt on the importance of play for children. We know that, far from wasting their time, it is in fact the way they get to grips with and make sense of the world. Play now constitutes a major part of Early Years education, although, sadly, today's target-driven mindset demands measurable goals and objectives even from our children's play time, just in case it fails to deliver satisfactorily.

To our focus-grouped, mission-statemented, purpose-driven culture, the fact that play might be important for adults too —might even be a means of deepening and enriching our faith—can be positively scary. Of course, we have Paul talking about putting aside 'the ways of childhood' (see 1 Corinthians 13:11), but we have to balance this with Jesus pointing out the need to 'become like little children' to enter the kingdom of heaven (see Matthew 18:3). We ought to reflect on whether we might sometimes learn very important things about ourselves, about God and what it means to follow him, by 'just mucking around'—that delightfully unfocused state of being that was allowed to fill so many school holidays in earlier decades.

If we marginalise children, we don't simply impoverish our own understanding of the kingdom; we run the risk of jeopardising their understanding of what it means to belong to the family of God. It is salutary to remember those rather less consoling words of Jesus, the ones about 'whoever causes one of these little ones to stumble' being better off if they were pushed off a bridge in concrete boots (I paraphrase a little: see Mark 9:42). This is not to say that we should start beating ourselves up over how materialistic our children are, and how much better it would be if their Christmas wish list comprised a bag of sweets, a tangerine and maybe a new pair of shoes if they were very lucky. We started these Advent readings by thinking about how the giving and receiving of gifts was endorsed by Jesus himself. What we do need to remember is that it is our responsibility to model to the children we know that seeking God's kingdom is of supreme importance—more important than presents, shopping, sport or even (whisper it) SATs.

## For reflection

*To what extent can we express playfulness in our worship? Do we allow space for the passionate, the disruptive, the messy, which may be an essential part of who God is?*

## 23 December

# PARADOX

In the beginning was the Word, and the Word was with God, and the Word was God. He was with God in the beginning. Through him all things were made; without him nothing was made that has been made. In him was life, and that life was the light of all people. The light shines in the darkness, and the darkness has not overcome it... The true light that gives light to everyone was coming into the world. He was in the world, and though the world was made through him, the world did not recognise him. He came to that which was his own, but his own did not receive him. Yet to all who did receive him, to those who believed in his name, he gave the right to become children of God... The Word became flesh and made his dwelling among us. We have seen his glory, the glory of the one and only [Son], who came from the Father, full of grace and truth.

JOHN 1:1–5, 9–12, 14

These sonorous words comprise the ninth and final lesson in a traditional Nine Lessons and Carols service, as held in so many churches and cathedrals at this season. Our cathedral is no exception and our band of pilgrims can enjoy the warm seasonal glow that accompanies post-carol service mingling over suitably festive refreshments. Choristers and clergy are receiving congratulations for their hard work in weaving together a moving and worshipful blend of music and words.

It so happens, however, that one of the Minor Canons feels a hand on their cassock sleeve and hears a plaintive voice asking, 'That last bit from the Bible—can you possibly explain to me what it was all about?'

We may be faithful attenders at carol services and have heard these words read every year, for more years than we care to remember, without ever stopping to ask ourselves whether we have a clue what the Gospel writer was attempting to say. As well as the simplicity of 'letting the children come', which we considered yesterday, and the nativity accoutrements of stable, donkey and star, we have here the mind-bending abstractions of the incarnation—a seeming impossibility, a paradox.

These Gospel verses speak of the pre-existent Word being with God, and at the same time being God. The Word is the source of all life, there 'in the beginning', encompassing the universe and yet choosing to 'become flesh'. And as the birth narratives of Jesus Christ tell us, the Word did not take form as some kind of superman, but took up residence as a single cell in the womb of an unmarried Middle Eastern peasant girl, living centuries before any kind of antenatal health care. It sounds rather like one of those fairy stories where an immensely powerful magical being is tricked by the hero into transforming into a tiny creature, which the hero then imprisons or destroys.

In his provocatively titled book *Five Impossible Things to Believe Before Christmas*, Kevin Scully describes the Buddhist concept of the kōan: taking a seemingly absurd statement (such as 'the sound of one hand clapping') and meditating on it, silencing the senses in the hope of coming to a deeper understanding of life. He argues that 'pondering the incarnation as a kōan can be a powerful aid to faith... it becomes an act of detachment that can, ironically, lead to adoration'. Instead of approaching the incarnation as an intellectual proposition, which we must grasp fully with our rational faculties, we set aside reason and approach the mystery humbly. Then, Scully says, we are 'potentially at the threshold of a profound spiritual encounter'.[7]

While it is important to be able to give reasons for what we believe, to have a faith with strong bones of biblical understanding, nourished by sacramental encounter, rather than struggling along with a shapeless jelly of emotion, speculation and subjectivity, we must resist the temptation to feel that we have God safely sorted and boxed in the 'religion' section of life. If our God is truly infinite, we will never come to the end of him—but then again we come up against the paradox that 'the Word became flesh'. As we reflected last week, God became like us, so that we could begin to understand him a little more.

How can we attempt to get our heads around this? It reminds me a bit of my family's experience when we first moved to London. For the first few months we despaired of understanding the place we had come to. Where was London? Was it to be found at Piccadilly Circus? Buckingham Palace? St Paul's Cathedral? Then we met a kind man at a dinner party who explained that London was really a series of villages. Get to know your village, then the next one, and the next; travel in buses to see how the villages connect together—and suddenly you find you are beginning to understand the shape of London.

We get to know our little bit of God, taking the simple steps of faith that even a child can comprehend, but as we continue our exploration, we find there is more, and yet more. Instead of approaching such exploration with the expectations of a map maker or surveyor, aiming to catalogue and regulate all that we discover into a coherent and definitive body of knowledge, we have to be prepared to embrace the scary possibilities of paradox, even as we think we begin to understand. God, you see, is even bigger than London...

Many people tend to speak of the Bible as 'the Word of God'. Rather, scripture comprises words inspired by God that tell the story of his dealings with the human race. Our passage from John's gospel describes how Jesus is the Word, the *Logos*—a term drawn from ancient Greek philosophy and used by some to denote a First Principle, the foundation of everything. He is Meaning, just as God revealed himself to the covenant people in the Old Testament as Being.

When we think about salvation, we should not envisage it as simply a matter of signing up to some kind of heavenly statement of faith. After all, however precisely statements of faith are shaped, and however carefully chosen and closely argued the phrases are, words so easily prove slippery and subversive, shifting their meaning the longer we reflect on them, until we start to wonder what exactly it is they are trying to say. At the end of the day, the Christian hope of salvation means accepting the truth of God with us, taking up the unbelievable offer of relationship with the heavenly Father as demonstrated in the life of Jesus 2000 years ago. We can start to take steps of faith even if we don't understand exactly what we are doing or why.

Better still, however, we are not limited to struggling to understand the meaning of events of two millennia ago. Through the action, here and now, of the Holy Spirit, we can access, here and now, the person and power of God, as we receive tokens of his love in the bread and wine of Holy

Communion. Following the injunction of the psalmist (34:8), we can 'taste and see that the Lord is good'.

## For reflection

'There is in God (some say) a deep but dazzling darkness...'
HENRY VAUGHAN (1622–95)

## 24 December

# MOST HOLY NIGHT

The people walking in darkness have seen a great light; on those living in the land of deep darkness a light has dawned. You have enlarged the nation and increased their joy; they rejoice before you as people rejoice at the harvest, as soldiers rejoice when dividing the plunder. For as in the day of Midian's defeat, you have shattered the yoke that burdens them, the bar across their shoulders, the rod of their oppressor. Every warrior's boot used in battle and every garment rolled in blood will be destined for burning, will be fuel for the fire. For to us a child is born, to us a son is given, and the government will be on his shoulders. And he will be called Wonderful Counsellor, Mighty God, Everlasting Father, Prince of Peace. Of the increase of his government and peace there will be no end. He will reign on David's throne and over his kingdom, establishing and upholding it with justice and righteousness from that time on and for ever. The zeal of the Lord Almighty will accomplish this.

ISAIAH 9:2–7

After the exuberance of the nativity play and the pageantry of the big carol service, the midnight Communion service of Christmas Eve can feel dramatically different. While many congregations work hard to put on a full choral production with processions, bells, smells, candles, banners, crosses and anything else they can find in the vestry, others choose to build a contrasting atmosphere. After all, this is when we remember how a very particular baby was born—coming, as babies so often choose to come—during the hours of darkness, when the mother has finally stopped rushing around (riding donkeys to Bethlehem, for example) and is at rest. Personally, I feel it is a time for stillness, watchfulness, quiet meditation, so bright lights and full-on celebration seem out of place.

Whether the service begins at midnight or is timed to finish just as the bells signal the first minutes of the new day, a moment comes when people can at last wish each other a Happy Christmas before hurrying home to check that all is ready for the celebrations later on. Stepping out after them into our cathedral close, in the relative quiet of Christmas night, can we pilgrims catch any sense of wonder, anything remotely resembling seasonal magic—or is that purely the preserve of children, leaning surreptitiously from their bedroom windows to glimpse Santa on his sleigh? What do the events we remember this night truly signify?

Our Bible reading, the third of the Nine Lessons from the carol service, promises us nothing less than universal liberation and national transformation. Like yesterday's opening verses from John's Gospel, the words can wash over us in a tide of poetry—a great light for the people walking in darkness… to us a child is born… Prince of Peace. It is easy to overlook the harsh imagery of plundering soldiers, warriors' boots and bloodstained clothes.

The prophet's vision is one of liberation from political oppression, release from a dreadful era of warfare and suffering. The promise is of a leader beyond imagining, one who will take power not to further his own ends but to bring justice and righteousness, wielding governance so strong and stable that it will endure beyond all expectation, as will the peace that he establishes. This speaks of one greater than Gandhi, Gorbachev or Mandela, one greater than Caesar Augustus, greater even than David, greatest of Israel's kings. The rule of this Messiah (literally 'anointed one'—marked with holy oil as a sign of authority, as priests and monarchs still are today) will last for ever.

If we have never lived under harshly authoritarian rule or survived a time of war, it may be hard to grasp the full emotional force of this passage. To read of people rejoicing as 'at the harvest' does not make much impact on the super-market generation—but maybe some readers of this book have experienced at first hand the collective sigh of relief in a country after a peace accord ends the horrors of civil war, when weapons begin to be laid down (and are even turned into works of art, as happened in an amazingly imaginative church-sponsored project in Mozambique). Even if our lives have not been directly touched by such events, we can reflect on the fact that these prophetic words spoke to their original audience not of a folksy stable scene in a far-off future time but of the possibility of freedom from the immediate threat posed by the Assyrian Empire, most cruel of conquerors.

Sadly, a glance at human history reminds us that when one season of bloodshed is concluded, another is continuing—or beginning—somewhere else. Just as peace seems to be breaking out all over, a new tyrant is plotting a coup, and, as always, it is the little people, those simply trying to live their lives, rear their children and care for their elderly, who suffer the consequences. When my elder son spent four months in the now peaceful country of Rwanda, he visited memorial centres documenting the horrors of the 1994 genocide; he and his friends also gazed across Lake Kivu to the Democratic

Republic of the Congo, where (at least at the time of writing) armed and shockingly bloody conflict continues.

The promise of Christmas Eve, this most holy night, is that fundamental change is possible, however. The light has dawned on those living in 'the land of the shadow of death' (as the KJV picturesquely translates Isaiah 9:2). Human efforts, no matter how well intentioned, cannot bring about eternal peace and incorruptible justice, because of human selfishness and sin. There is only one who can bring the necessary hope and healing, the one who is both God and man. His touch will restore the brokenness not only of humankind but of the whole of creation, repairing the effects of the original rebellion of those who were supposed to be stewards and caretakers, but chose to take what they wanted, when they wanted. Their children have, with few exceptions, chosen to do the same ever since.

If this is what God can do, are we ready to trust him to work his holy magic in our lives, in our churches, our communities? Has it occurred to us that for his power to be unleashed, we may have to offer ourselves as the means by which his zeal can work? Then we will see discord become harmony, wastelands blooming, brokenness made so whole that we can barely glimpse the lines of mending.

## Reflection

'The wolf will live with the lamb, the leopard will lie down with the goat, the calf and the lion and the yearling together; and a little child will lead them. The cow will feed with the bear, their young will lie down together, and the lion will eat straw like the ox. Infants will play near the hole of the cobra; young children will put their hands into the viper's nest. They will neither harm nor *destroy on all my holy mountain, for the earth will be filled with the knowledge of the Lord as the waters cover the sea'* (Isaiah 11:6–9).

*٭*

## 25 December

# IS THAT IT?

And there were shepherds living out in the fields near by, keeping watch over their flocks at night. An angel of the Lord appeared to them, and the glory of the Lord shone around them, and they were terrified. But the angel said to them, 'Do not be afraid. I bring you good news of great joy that will be for all the people. Today in the town of David a Saviour has been born to you; he is the Messiah, the Lord. This will be a sign to you: you will find a baby wrapped in cloths and lying in a manger.' Suddenly a great company of the heavenly host appeared with the angel, praising God and saying, 'Glory to God in the highest heaven, and on earth peace to those on whom his favour rests.' When the angels had left them... the shepherds said to one another, 'Let's go to Bethlehem and see this thing that has happened, which the Lord has told us about.' So they hurried off and found Mary and Joseph, and the baby, who was lying in the manger. When they had seen him, they spread the word concerning what had been told them about this child, and all who heard it were amazed.

LUKE 2:8–18 (ABRIDGED)

Our reading for today is customarily the seventh lesson of the carol service, and the story it tells means that we start our reflection in the dark, well before Christmas sunrise. If we have young children, we may be rather more familiar with this hour than we would wish, as well as with the inevitable argument about whether 4.30am is too early to start unwrapping presents. There are still a few hours to go until dawn—but if we pilgrims find ourselves wakeful, and fancy stepping out to look at the fading stars, we will see those people who have yet to go to bed. Duty still calls for the police officer on patrol, for the ambulance crew rushing an indisposed reveller to A&E, for the minicab drivers on the late shift. Beyond the city, there will be those already up this morning, as on every morning of the year, to look after their livestock.

Imagine what would happen, then, if the skies suddenly split open like a spectacular special effects shot from a science fiction blockbuster, and the glory of the Lord was revealed, causing ambulance drivers to swerve, police officers to shield their eyes, minicab drivers to drop their coffee mugs and everyone to stare open-mouthed. That is more or less what happened on the night of Jesus' birth. And, of course, the shepherds on the Bethlehem hills had no idea that that particular night was in any way special. As they kept their usual chilly and boring vigil with the sheep, they were not expecting any kind of visitation, let alone an angelic one.

This is my favourite of the episodes surrounding Jesus' birth. It is breathtaking in scope, recklessly extravagant—'a great company of the heavenly host'! Why not just a single magnificent angel, like the one who appeared separately to Mary and Joseph? Why did these shepherds deserve such a revelation of glory? It is a theophany as splendid as anything from the Sinai era, as awe-inspiring as the times when the *Shekinah*, the Hebrew name for the bright cloud of God's presence, descended on the tabernacle in the wilderness (see Numbers 9:15–16) and later at the dedication of the

Jerusalem temple (see 2 Chronicles 7:1–3). Understandably, these men were scared witless.

Then surprise is piled on surprise: the sign that the shepherds must seek to verify the coming of the Saviour is 'a baby wrapped in cloths and lying in a manger'. You can almost imagine little thought bubbles floating above their heads, amid the swirling splendour of the heavens—'WHAT??' Clearly God knew what he was about in choosing these first witnesses to the incarnation, however, as they did not try to puzzle out exactly what the angel meant. When everything was quiet once more, they probably turned to one another and shrugged. It was clearly the Lord who had arranged this event, so what could they do but obey the angel's command? Sometimes too much thought, too desperate an attempt to get it all straight in our heads before we act, is not what God requires of us.

It is undeniable, though, that we can fall victim to a certain 'Is that it?' feeling about Christmas, especially as we get older and have managed to work out who fills the stockings. A friend once commented to me that he found the most depressing point of the year to be that post-Christmas dinner hour when the food had been eaten and the presents opened, so that the day offered no further possibilities beyond a chilly family walk. That was it: Christmas over for another year.

What my friend needed was an effort of imagination, a reminder to himself that—as we saw in the very first week of our reflections—although feasting and gifts are not to be piously denigrated as 'worldly', at the same time we must not forget what they symbolise. It's easy to say, yet easy to forget. In fact, we could go so far as to describe our Christmas celebration as a sacrament, the visible sign of a heavenly reality, our small way of participating in the rejoicing of the angels that the hope of God with us has come true. By extension, we may well be called to do what we can to ensure that 'all the people' get the chance to celebrate too, to participate in the banquet.

The story of the shepherds shows how the incarnation meant that God's glory burst out everywhere; it was not limited to the worthy, the conspicuously holy and the enlightened (a theme that runs throughout Luke's Gospel). It was—and is—good news of great joy for absolutely everybody, including those on the margins, who may lack the cushioning relationships with family and friends that protect so many of us through the bumpier bits of life. If not this year, then perhaps next year, some of us may be called to think for the first time about planning a celebration that includes at least one person from the edge of our community. We need to tread sensitively and avoid rushing in with patronising benevolence—but it may be that until now we have always chosen to duck this particular challenge.

Returning to our pilgrim sojourn at the cathedral, it so happens that the Dean (chief cleric of the cathedral team) is a person of enormous kindness and generosity, qualities undiminished by the exhausting round of pre-Christmas services. Thus it is that as midday approaches, the cathedral doors are thrown open wide and volunteers serve a festival dinner to an astonishingly varied selection of local people. Let us sit and eat with them, with gratitude and an appropriate amount of greed, for the food is both plentiful and free.

## Prayer

*For what we have received, Lord, help us to be truly thankful.*

*

## 26 December

# THE FEAST OF STEPHEN

[Stephen said to the Sanhedrin] 'You stiff-necked people! Your hearts and ears are still uncircumcised. You are just like your ancestors: you always resist the Holy Spirit! Was there ever a prophet your ancestors did not persecute? They even killed those who predicted the coming of the Righteous One...' When the members of the Sanhedrin heard this, they were furious... But Stephen, full of the Holy Spirit, looked up to heaven and saw the glory of God, and Jesus standing at the right hand of God. 'Look,' he said, 'I see heaven open and the Son of Man standing at the right hand of God.' At this they covered their ears and, yelling at the top of their voices, they all rushed at him, dragged him out of the city and began to stone him. Meanwhile, the witnesses laid their coats at the feet of a young man named Saul. While they were stoning him, Stephen prayed, 'Lord Jesus, receive my spirit.' Then he fell on his knees and cried out, 'Lord, do not hold this sin against them.' When he had said this, he fell asleep.

ACTS 7:51–60 (ABRIDGED)

How many people remember this feast in these hazy post-Christmas days? I would love to know how many churches dedicated to St Stephen actually celebrate their special day, the festival of their patron saint. If we give the matter a bit of thought, we may recall that Good King Wenceslas, the tenth-century Duke of Bohemia, legendarily went out 'on the feast of Stephen... when the snow lay round about, deep and crisp and even', in order to deliver fuel, food and wine to a poverty-stricken peasant, and his saintly footsteps were so warm that they stopped his whingeing companion from freezing. Today's commemoration of the Feast of Stephen is more likely to feature a meal involving recycled turkey, visits to far-flung relatives and a trip to town for a first assault on the sales.

Turning to the account of the real Stephen's death is a brutal wake-up call. Welcome to the full and shockingly mortal consequences of following the way of the Christ-child! We may personally consider the pattern of the Church calendar to be hopelessly anachronistic here: why place such a significant commemoration on a day so dedicated to prolonging seasonal cheer? There are few people likely to want to come to church today, after so many special services, especially if the worship is planned with so downbeat a focus as a young man's death. Let's be open to a different agenda, though. We have reflected on how God's glory burst open the created order in the events of the incarnation; here are some other consequences of that outbursting—disruption, mess, suffering, untimely death.

In the peaceful little cathedral on our own pilgrimage, we can forget that so many places of worship have been associated with violent death. The body of King Edmund of East Anglia, killed by Danish invaders in the ninth century, became the focus of the great abbey at the town now known as Bury St Edmunds; the church of St Alphege in Greenwich, south London, is reputedly on the site where the Anglo-Saxon bishop was beaten to death by foreign raiders in 1012; Archbishop Thomas Becket was murdered by Henry II's men in Canterbury Cathedral, where his shrine became an enormously popular site of pilgrimage until the dissolution of the monasteries.

Stephen, the first believer to die for his faith, is described earlier in Acts as 'a man full of God's grace and power' who 'performed great wonders and signs among the people' (6:8). At his very first appearance (v. 5), he is named as one of the seven new leaders chosen by the original twelve apostles to help with the growing ministry. There, Stephen is characterised as 'full of faith and of the Holy Spirit', definitely somebody to have around and on your side as the work of building the Church gathers pace. After his arrest on manufactured charges of blasphemy, his boldly uncompromising speech to the Jewish authorities proves to be his death warrant. As biblical scholar Loveday Alexander describes it, 'Stephen's final words... crackle with the pain of the "parting of the ways" between church and synagogue. Seen from the other side of that divide, it's a despairing indictment of the failures of God's chosen people to recognise the work of the Holy Spirit.'

In passing, it is worth noting her later caveat that Stephen's quarrel was not with the Law of Moses itself, but with those who failed to keep it: 'We cannot transfer Stephen's bitter denunciation of a particular group in his own context to a post-"parting" perspective, as if what Stephen says here is meant to be true of all Jews everywhere... in a post-Holocaust world it is not a stance that Christians can accept.'[8]

The method of execution suffered by Stephen was public, painful and excruciatingly slow (pause and think about it for a moment, if you can bear to do so). According to tradition, cruel deaths were the lot of all but one of the twelve apostles, John alone (of whom we will read tomorrow) surviving to old age. It is in some ways a chilling experience to visit the splendidly preserved Roman amphitheatre in Pula, Croatia, when you reflect that Christians were among those held in the underground passageways, ready to be brought out to be torn apart by wild animals for the entertainment of the crowds. As Tertullian of Carthage (c.160–c.225) is remembered as writing, 'the blood of the martyrs is the seed of the church'. In some ways, this echoes the sombre words of Jesus: 'Unless a grain of wheat falls to the ground and dies, it remains only a single seed. But if it dies, it produces many seeds' (John 12:24).

'Martyr' has come to mean 'somebody who dies for what they believe in', but the original Greek word simply meant 'witness', one who was prepared to testify in a court of law about what they believed to be true. Stephen's status as a witness led to his death because of the unpalatable nature (as far as the Sanhedrin was concerned) of what he held to be true. At the same time, his willingness to submit to an agonising and humiliating death witnessed to the crowd of the unshakeable conviction of his faith. Among that crowd, looking after the coats of those who had grown hot and sweaty hurling rocks, was a young man by the name of Saul. He not only approved of the killing but was inspired to embark on his own campaign of persecution against the new believers. Subsequent events proved beyond all expectation the truth of Jesus' words from John's Gospel, however. The death of Stephen was the single seed that, through the conversion of Saul the persecutor into Paul the apostle, became the means of the Church seeding itself across the known world, borne on the wind of the Spirit.

## *For reflection*

*'Therefore, since we are surrounded by such a great cloud of witnesses, let us throw off everything that hinders and the sin that so easily entangles. And let us run with perseverance the race marked out for us, fixing our eyes on Jesus, the pioneer and perfecter of faith' (Hebrews 12:1–2).*

*

## 27 December

# JESUS' BEST FRIEND

That which was from the beginning, which we have heard, which we have seen with our eyes, which we have looked at and our hands have touched—this we proclaim concerning the Word of life. The life appeared; we have seen it and testify to it, and we proclaim to you the eternal life, which was with the Father and has appeared to us. We proclaim to you what we have seen and heard, so that you also may have fellowship with us. And our fellowship is with the Father and with his Son, Jesus Christ. We write this to make our joy complete. This is the message we have heard from him and declare to you: God is light; in him there is no darkness at all. If we claim to have fellowship with him and yet walk in the darkness, we lie and do not live out the truth. But if we walk in the light, as he is in the light, we have fellowship with one another, and the blood of Jesus, his Son, purifies us from all sin.

1 JOHN 1:1–7

For many people, today marks the end of the Christmas holiday. The work routine begins again, with the prospect of a further short break to mark the New Year. Our virtual pilgrimage continues on towards Epiphany, and we have lingered at the manger long enough. Now it is time to make a start on the route that will eventually lead us home. This does not mean that the next part of the way is to be hurried over, however. The homeward journey—and even what happens after the final return—is as significant a part of the experience as the original departing. Author and pilgrimage leader Andrew Jones spells out this special characteristic of being a pilgrim: 'A pilgrimage never finishes. The return home is often the new beginning of lasting relationships and the process of relating and story telling… a pilgrimage is all about the preparing, the travelling and the returning.'[9] We will find there is more to learn, more to encounter, in the days still to come.

It's time to leave our cathedral, but, as we go, we pass the eagle lectern, the statuesque brass stand (buffed to a gleam by a team of people who, I feel, ought to be identified as ladies; I have yet to meet a gentleman who voluntarily polishes church brass) holding a supersized Bible. The eagle is the symbol of St John, whose feast day falls today, another of those post-Christmas commemorations so easily overlooked.

Scholarly debate continues as to whether St John the Apostle and St John the Epistle and Gospel writer were the same person. There is further dispute over whether either character was the same as John of Patmos, author of the apocalyptic book of Revelation, because the somewhat more rough-and-ready Greek of the latter gives the impression of having little in common with the elaborate cadences of John's Gospel. Some might argue that if John wrote Revelation in exile on the island of Patmos, after a series of shattering visions experienced in a cave, the style might well be a bit less finished than that of the Gospel, which some scholars think was composed in the infinitely more salubrious surroundings of the city of Ephesus. The traditional view is that the Gospel, the apocalypse and the letters of 1, 2 and 3 John were all written by John, brother of James, son of Zebedee, former Galilean fisherman—and, for simplicity's sake, let's go with the traditional view for now.

John was one of the most prominent of Jesus' disciples. Along with Peter and James, he was one of the witnesses to the drama of the mountaintop transfiguration (Mark 9:2–13). Luke names him, alongside Peter, as the disciple whom Jesus sent ahead into the city to prepare the setting for the Passover meal that became his last supper with his friends (Luke 22:9–13); Jesus then chose him, again with Peter and John, to watch and wait with him during the agonising hours in Gethsemane (Mark 14:32–42), a vigil that they sadly failed to keep.

In John's Gospel, we find a different and surprisingly intimate tone compared with the other Gospels: there is no mention of 'John' but instead references to 'the disciple whom Jesus loved'. This is one who relaxed against Jesus at the last supper (John 13:23–25) and ran faster than Peter to reach the empty tomb first on Easter morning (20:3–8), where he 'saw and believed'. Most poignantly, we find him standing alongside the women at the foot of the cross (19:25–27), where Jesus, in his agony, asks him to take on the responsibility of caring for his mother Mary. While nothing can be conclusively proved, it is possible to take a trip to Turkey (which I warmly recommend anyway) and visit the restored remains of a small stone house that, over the centuries, has been named as the final home of Mary, just a short distance from Ephesus and also not far from where the supposed burial place of John himself is located.

'The disciple whom Jesus loved': we should pause on this thought, and dwell on it. There was a disciple that Jesus actually loved—the word used being *agape*, which has connotations of an esteem characterised by self-sacrifice, but which can also imply straightforward, warm affection. Even

Jesus needed a special and particular friend, one closer to him even than Peter, generally the most enthusiastic and voluble of the Twelve. It is noteworthy, too, that this emotional vulnerability is recorded in the Gospel that often seems to portray the Saviour as perpetually calm, cool and purposeful, even at the point of death.

True and deep friendship, soul-to-soul camaraderie, could become an endangered art in a society as obsessed as ours is with both romantic love and the many dimensions of sexual expression. It can also end up squeezed by all the other conflicting pressures on our time—work, more work, family life both nuclear and extended, keeping fit, and of course the plethora of activities associated with church life. Even so, friendship remains an essential component of a healthy and vigorous emotional life, whether we are a party animal or a hermit, committed to a carefully chosen few or freely shared with many, in a lifelong committed relationship or single.

Opening ourselves to others carries risk, it is true: friends can hurt and forsake us as well as be a source of love and nurture. But John's gentle words in our Bible passage today provide a secure foundation for building relationships within the body of Christ: 'If we walk in the light, as [God] is in the light, we have fellowship with one another, and the blood of Jesus, his Son, purifies us from all sin.' Thanks to the great light that dawned at the first Christmas and has never disappeared, there is no need for us ever again to stumble along in the dark, lonely and anxious. The Word, the Son of God, brings cleansing from sin, eternal life and illumination for our daily walk, so that we can hope for the growth of true fellowship with one another and so taste a joy that is brought to completion in him.

## For reflection

'Though one may be overpowered, two can defend themselves. A cord of three strands is not quickly broken' (Ecclesiastes 4:12).

*

## 28 December

# THE HOLY INNOCENTS

When [the Magi] had gone, an angel of the Lord appeared to Joseph in a dream. 'Get up,' he said, 'take the child and his mother and escape to Egypt. Stay there until I tell you, for Herod is going to search for the child to kill him.' So he got up, took the child and his mother during the night and left for Egypt, where he stayed until the death of Herod. And so was fulfilled what the Lord had said through the prophet: 'Out of Egypt I called my son.' When Herod realised that he had been outwitted by the Magi, he was furious, and he gave orders to kill all the boys in Bethlehem and its vicinity who were two years old and under, in accordance with the time he had learned from the Magi. Then what was said through the prophet Jeremiah was fulfilled: 'A voice is heard in Ramah, weeping and great mourning, Rachel weeping for her children and refusing to be comforted, because they are no more.'

MATTHEW 2:13–18

As we step out through the West Door of our cathedral, let's look back one last time. The interior is, it has to be said, on the dim side (the next stage of the ongoing restoration programme will focus on the electrics), but the edge of shadowiness means that the stands of votive candles seem to burn more brightly. Rows of tealights flicker in the small but perpetual draught (insulation coming after electrics on the 'to do' list). Each one represents a petition of some kind, unanswered or answered, and the written prayers on the adjacent board present a sprinkling of thanks and praise amid a litany of grim medical prognoses, broken relationships, miscarriages and redundancies. The little dancing lights are mostly desperate pleas for help and healing, for comfort and stamina in a journey through the valley of the shadow.

Today, 28 December, is the feast of the Holy Innocents, the day for remembering the boy babies and toddlers murdered by order of Herod the Great. Once again, the Church calendar diverts our attention from happy holidays and bids us think on suffering—suffering that was the consequence of calculated wickedness. Moving on ahead to the events commemorated by Epiphany, today's feast recalls the part of the Gospel story where the Magi, the wise men (who were not kings and didn't come in threes), have arrived in Jerusalem and made the mistake of alerting the ageing tyrant Herod to their search for a new king of the Jews (Matthew 2:2). Angry at the failure of his plan to dupe the visitors into revealing the child's whereabouts, Herod decides on the slaughter of male infants not only in Bethlehem but in the surrounding settlements.

There is no record of this episode except the one found in Matthew's Gospel. Some say that this is because the massacre was not horrific enough to warrant special mention, given the overall context of Herod's reign, which was littered with atrocities. Getting rid of potential rivals, by whatever means necessary, has been pretty much standard behaviour for kings throughout history. Estimates of the number of boys killed by Herod have varied enormously, from thousands to barely a dozen—but even if one child was murdered in this way, the irony is appalling. The Christ-child, come to save the world, ends up being the unwitting cause of bitter loss.

Why, in heaven's name, did God not intervene? Surely it would have been an opportune moment for Herod to suffer a fatal heart attack, for the occupying Roman forces to choose to get rid of the old monster and put somebody else on the throne. Maybe, just maybe, God did intervene, however, through the actions of those men and women who were willing to endanger themselves by offering protection to those at risk. Perhaps a kindly farmer hid a couple of youngsters under a heap of hay in his stable; perhaps an older woman snatched a baby from his mother and concealed him under her robe. Perhaps there were those whose memories of that terrible day were narratives of rescue, of unlooked-for help and salvation.

When faced with horror, we are likely to feel overwhelmed, like helpless bystanders who can do nothing except deplore what is happening and try to protect ourselves and those whom we love most. The alternative is to do what we can to make a difference, no matter how inadequate it may seem. This will involve disregarding, if possible, the likely cost to us personally. A while ago, I was moved by the story of Marie Ozanne, a Salvation Army leader in Guernsey during the Second World War. She dared to complain to the German occupation forces about their treatment of Russian slave labourers brought to the Channel Islands, some of whom were only teenagers. As a result, she herself was imprisoned, dying a few months after her release at the age of 38; her courageous actions are barely remembered today, although in 1947 the Salvation Army posthumously awarded her their highest honour for 'a self-sacrificing concern for men's freedom to serve God and for the saving of others'.[10]

No matter how many are saved, however, the dead are irreplaceable, their unique genetic code wiped from the planet for ever. The massacres remembered by the names of places such as Dunblane, Columbine and Beslan are remembered as events of particular monstrosity because parents generally assume that they will live to see their children grow up. It is offensive to think that there might be any easy answers or quick consolations in the face of such trauma. In his Gospel, Matthew notes that these events are the grim fulfilment of words from the prophet Jeremiah (31:15); the original context was the catastrophe of exile, but here they remind us that it is permissible to grieve without trying to slot events into some kind of divine plan, declaring in the words of Romans 8:28 that 'in all things God works for the good of those who love him' while we can barely see for tears.

Christians (just like other human beings) are allowed to cry, to howl with anguish, to lose it completely. The desolate places of grief are not to be rushed through according to somebody else's prescription of psychological stages. Jesus was so upset by the death of his friend Lazarus (John 11:33) that, according to the nuances of the Greek word used, he was literally shaking with emotion, groaning aloud. We, then, should put out of our minds any idea that there might be prizes for 'coping well' and not 'making a fuss'. And when we come alongside those who are enduring loss, we will find that silence—not blessed soundbites—may well be the only appropriate response.

## For reflection

'When [Job's three friends] saw him from a distance, they could hardly recognise him; they began to weep aloud, and they tore their robes and sprinkled dust on their heads. Then they sat on *the ground with him for seven days and seven nights. No one said a word to him, because they saw how great his suffering was'* (Job 2:12–13).

# Travelling into tomorrow

These days are still part of the Twelve Days of Christmas, which come to an end on 5 January, giving way to the season of Epiphany. It is not yet time to bundle up Christmas and clear it away for another year, along with the wilting tree, the discarded wrapping paper, the cards and the unwanted gifts (earmarked for tactful disposal). This is a time for continued reflection on and special thanksgiving for the miracle of the incarnation, for exploring still further the implications of the first Christmas. In the middle comes New Year, not an ostensibly Christian celebration, but still the second highlight of this time of year for most people. It prompts us to think about our plans, hopes and fears for the months ahead, and later this week we will consider how the tradition of New Year resolutions can prove helpful as we ready ourselves for the future, while still being open to the likelihood of God surprising us.

On our virtual pilgrimage, we continue homewards. As in any return home after an emotional or spiritual 'high', we may fear forgetting the lessons we have learned for our ongoing faith journey—the sense of God's special closeness that we have experienced, that unexpected healing with which we have been blessed. We should not harbour such worries, however. The Lord God promises to be with his people: as we read in Psalm 125:2, 'As the mountains surround Jerusalem, so the Lord surrounds his people both now and for evermore', and he who continued to accompany the Israelites through the desert, despite their infuriating habits of complaining and disobedience, will not abandon us. We will not leave him behind as we return, nor do we have to imagine him waiting for our eventual arrival in some ethereal realm. He walks beside us, even though we may not recognise him, as the disciples on the Emmaus road did not recognise Jesus after the resurrection (see Luke 24:13–35).

No two journeys—whether a stroll in the park, a pilgrimage or a journey of the heart—are exactly the same, even if we try to follow the same route as previously. Of course, the surroundings (metaphorical or literal) may have changed, the weather grown better or worse, but we will have changed too, if only because we have grown a little older. Our circumstances move on, our perceptions develop, and this new journey (like every journey we take) will lead us a further distance along the path of discipleship. For some, that will mean drawing even closer to God. For others, sadly, their choices may mark the beginning of a growing distance in that relationship, for whatever reason.

*

*29 December*

# THE LONG WAY HOME

The devil took [Jesus] to the holy city and set him on the highest point of the temple. 'If you are the Son of God,' he said, 'throw yourself down. For it is written: "He will command his angels concerning you, and they will lift you up in their hands, so that you will not strike your foot against a stone."' Jesus answered him, 'It is also written: "Do not put the Lord your God to the test."' Again, the devil took him to a very high mountain and showed him all the kingdoms of the world and their splendour. 'All this I will give you,' he said, 'if you will bow down and worship me.' Jesus said to him, 'Away from me, Satan! For it is written: "Worship the Lord your God, and serve him only."' Then the devil left him, and angels came and attended him.

MATTHEW 4:5–11

On the homeward journey, some of us will be tempted to look for short cuts. After all, we have made it to the manger—pilgrimage destination achieved, cathedral gift shop raided, box ticked—and now it's time to move on briskly to the finish. While some love the slow unfolding of process, the indefinite delay of final decisions, others live for the thrill of completion. Teams or pilgrimage groups composed solely of one type or the other will soon run into problems; you need a balance of decision makers and evaluators in any selection of people in order to function effectively.

The 21st century is not generally conducive to the 'slow unfolding' approach. While the pace of life has been quickening ever since the Industrial Revolution, our era of instant communication, live comment and response, means that we are more inclined than ever to take the faster option, the no-fuss, minimal effort solution. One of the hard lessons involved in serious illness is the amount of waiting involved: waiting for referral (even if waiting lists are now shorter than in the past), waiting for tests, waiting for results, waiting for treatment, waiting for more tests and more results, and waiting for the return to health. Media commentators regularly deplore the attitudes generated by phenomena such as fast food, speed-dating and budget air travel, yearning for the days of home-cooked casseroles, courtship à la Jane Austen and ocean liners. At least the British still do queuing—up to a point.

The church, too, is not immune to the 'I want it here and I want it now' mindset. Church planting initiatives are generally a wonderful thing, bringing life, energy and witness to places of worship that are in terminal decline or altogether defunct. The downside of the planting mentality, however, is that we can end up dismissing as ineffectual the slow building up of a church over many years, which may well produce a stronger, more locally rooted congregation in the longer term. On a personal level, Christians can be inclined to expect healing or blessing or equipping for ministry at the touch of a hand or the sign of a cross. Of course God can provide in this way (he can do anything he likes) but, being God, he will act on his terms and in his timescale, not in deference to our self-centred demands.

Our Bible passage shows Jesus in the wilderness, tempted at the outset of his ministry to take short cuts to success.

The one attempting to lure him with suggestions of signs and wonders and instant world domination is named as the accuser or enemy. This is what the Hebrew word 'satan' means; it should not evoke images of a 'prince of darkness' in a swirling black cloak (red satin lining compulsory), nor yet a character with the horns, tail and terrifying grin of medieval iconography, but the wheedling, ultra-persuasive voice that tells lies and more lies, to try to distract us from the gentle whisper of God. Interestingly, the Greek equivalent, *diabolos*, which gives us 'devil' in these verses from Matthew, can also be an adjective meaning 'given to malicious gossip', something that few would consider 'diabolical' in the modern sense of the word.

Whether or not we believe in a personal devil, it is undeniable that the wheedling voice to which Jesus responds here in the wilderness takes much the same line as the voice that addressed Eve back in the garden of Eden. 'Yes, yes, I know what you have been told,' it coaxes. 'But I have a better suggestion, which really is in keeping with your best interests, honest.' Jesus resists the devil's temptations—well, that's to be expected, isn't it? He is the perfect Son of God, after all.

Interestingly, we are so familiar with the end of this story that we are unlikely to dwell on the fact that two of the accuser's suggestions were actually rather good ones. Turning stones into bread (see v. 3), for example, meant that Jesus would feel a whole lot better after his long fast. Nobody else would know what he had done—and hadn't Elijah the prophet enjoyed a miraculous delivery of bread in the desert (1 Kings 19:6; see also 17:2–6, cited earlier)? As for Jesus throwing himself off the temple in Jerusalem, that would provide an unforgettable spectacle, bringing the city to a standstill and proving God's power to the Roman authorities as well as to the Jewish community. Time would be short enough as it was, once Jesus' messianic claims became known, so a quick and dramatic start was essential. Thinking about it, why didn't Jesus start preaching until he was 30? His precocious theological insights were recognised when he was twelve (Luke 2:41–51), so why did God not fast-track him? After all, the salvation of the world was at stake.

History, however, is littered with stories of precocious children whose promise faded before they reached maturity or whose gifts were exhausted before they could be more than novelties. The boy Jesus, miracle worker, is the star of the apocryphal Infancy Gospel of Thomas. When compiling the documents that would form the New Testament, the early Church rightly rejected such stories of a show-off, priggish child, but they can serve as a warning of what might have been, if Jesus' parents had been pushy, if Mary had filled her son's head with stories of his astonishing birth instead of wisely keeping her thoughts to herself (see Luke 2:19). There were no short cuts for Jesus, but the slow passing of years in the routine of the carpentry trade meant that when his time finally came, he was ready—body, mind and heart.

As our pilgrim group makes its way through the residential side streets, away from the cathedral, we should notice the front gardens. So often a highlight of so many British neighbourhoods, with their seasonal rotation of dahlias and daffodils (or unchanging display of gravel and spiky grasses, if the garden architects have come calling), they are not looking their best at the butt-end of December, but they are not dead, only dormant. The bulbs have yet to appear, the buds are still tiny, and when the time is right, all their promise will unfold.

## Reflection

'Let us not become weary in doing good, for at the proper time we will reap a harvest if we do not give up' (Galatians 6:9).

*

## 30 December

# KNOWING THE BEST ROAD TO TAKE

Listen, my sons, to a father's instruction; pay attention, and gain understanding. I give you sound learning, so do not forsake my teaching. For I too was a son to my father, still tender, and cherished by my mother. Then he taught me, and he said to me, 'Take hold of my words with all your heart; keep my commands, and you will live. Get wisdom, get understanding; do not forget my words or turn away from them... Listen, my son, accept what I say, and the years of your life will be many. I instruct you in the way of wisdom and lead you along straight paths. When you walk, your steps will not be hampered; when you run, you will not stumble.'

PROVERBS 4:1–5, 10–12

Even if we have resolutely decided against short cuts, there will be times when we are unsure which road to take. We know our final destination, but we may end up struggling to work out the best route to get there. It's not even a matter of coming to a crossroads, where a choice is pressing, but of noticing that there is the option of a different road. The question at stake is whether 'different' also means 'better'— or not. One member of our group may argue fervently for the obscure side road that will apparently lead to an attractively quiet route to the coast where, over these final few days, our pilgrim path will come to an end; others will be stalwart advocates of sticking with the noisy but otherwise straightforward route bordering the dual carriageway.

In the choosing of roads, whether real or metaphorical, some tend to assume that the best option must be (in the overquoted words of Robert Frost) 'the one less travelled by', which will make 'all the difference'. We should bear in mind, though, that it may actually be less travelled because it is not a particularly good road. As the map reader in our marriage, I have led my long-suffering husband along many 'scenic routes'—single-track lanes with occasional monster tractors hurtling through, oblivious of the family car round the next bend. He still trembles at the memory of having to reverse a considerable distance along a hair-pin unfenced mountain road in the Pyrenees, when we found the way ahead blocked by a team resurfacing the crumbling tarmac.

On the other hand, we should not assume that, because we are on the road that our parents took or our friends or colleagues have taken, it is the best one for us. Rather than being a reasonable argument for continuity, 'it's what we've always done' can mean little more than a failure of imagination. We cannot imagine something being different; therefore we will argue that it cannot be so—just because. Of course there is a case to be made for maintaining values, for stability, for helping people to know where they are. At the same time, this must be balanced with openness to newness, difference and change.

Our choice of road has to be informed by more than personal whim or untested assumptions; such choices call for wisdom, the theme that we first considered on 17 December. In our Bible passage today, we hear a father telling his son how he gained wisdom from his own father, which he now wants to pass on so that his son's path through life will be smoother than otherwise. This process has much in common with what we now know as mentoring, a practice that has become hugely popular both in the church and in the wider community. These days, such a relationship is likely to be established outside the context of home and family, so that the one who is being mentored can reflect freely on every area of life. The aim of this ongoing reflection is to nurture a combination of self-awareness and God-awareness, with wisdom as one of the most important fruits of the whole process.

Without self-awareness, we are highly likely to end up stumbling through life, even falling down altogether. Deepening our awareness of who God is and how he is at work in the world is an essential part of Christian discipleship, but we also need to know ourselves, to be alert to the unconscious drives and influences that affect our choices and behaviour. We may be compelled to acknowledge these forces as the result of a sudden crisis, or we may come to recognise them after a prolonged period of heart-searching. Either way, we may eventually realise that although we had assumed we were conducting our lives as mature, independent individuals, we were in fact driven all along by pain from past hurts or by hunger for love, recognition, acceptance or peace. To begin the journey towards wholeness, we need to come to a point where we can acknowledge the existence, extent and strength of these hurts or hungers and admit that we need help and healing.

Retelling the story of our lives to ourselves and to others can be a way not only of tracing patterns of hurt but of discovering how God has been alongside us. We come to see how he was holding on to us, guiding us towards wholeness, even when we had no sense whatsoever of his presence, even when times felt very, very bad, when we felt most abandoned and hopeless. As we look back, especially if we do so prayerfully and with the help of a trusted adviser, we will start to recognise signs of God's abiding presence with us over the years. These signs may be moments as random as a passing encounter with a stranger, experiences as intangible as watching sunlight on water or listening to the wind in the trees, as well as insights that can be as unmistakably heaven-sent as opening the Bible and chancing upon a verse that resonates exactly with our situation.

If we make space for such recall, in due course we will find it begins to grow within us the wisdom that we need for the onward journey, even if at present we feel utterly inadequate and ill-equipped to continue on our way. In looking back, we may realise for the first time quite how many bad choices we made in the past (something that we will consider further tomorrow). We may already have such a low opinion of our own judgment that we dare not take a single step forward without the say-so of others. On the other hand, we may look back and find great encouragement in realising how decisions that we took with some trepidation turned out to be the best thing we could have done. It is our Father's hope, however, that every one of his children might grow to maturity, just as the long-ago father in the book of Proverbs hoped for his own child, and throughout the Bible we find the promise that wisdom is God's gift to us—all of us, not just the important, the powerful, the clever or the beautiful. We simply have to ask, with hearts and minds open to receive the gift, in whatever way it comes.

## *Reflection*

*'If any of you lacks wisdom, you should ask God, who gives generously to all without finding fault, and it will be given to you'* (James 1:5).

*

## 31 December

# NOWHERE

'Meaningless! Meaningless!' says the Teacher. 'Utterly meaning-less! Everything is meaningless.' What does anyone gain from all their labours at which they toil under the sun? Generations come and generations go, but the earth remains for ever. The sun rises and the sun sets, and hurries back to where it rises. The wind blows to the south and turns to the north; round and round it goes, ever returning on its course. All streams flow into the sea, yet the sea is never full. To the place the streams come from, there they return again. All things are wearisome, more than one can say… What has been will be again, what has been done will be done again; there is nothing new under the sun… There is no remembrance of people of old, and even those who are yet to come will not be remembered by those who follow them.

ECCLESIASTES 1:2–11 (ABRIDGED)

So much for agonising over which road to take: the choice has been made, the route followed, but, instead of finding a clear way ahead, our group of pilgrims is wandering in a bewildering sprawl of industrial estates. On the other side of giant *leylandii* hedges we can hear the roar of the ringroad, yet no matter how far we walk, we seem unable to escape the rows of identikit warehouses and offices, marooned in an expanse of tarmac. If our job was based here, we would no doubt walk through purposefully, conscious only of a neutral backdrop for the interior world of work. Ending up here by mistake, we find nothing to guide us, nowhere that looks like a way out. It is not even a scary wasteland of burned-out cars and broken glass, where we might at least feel a sense of heroism as we walk. This is nothing so much as boring.

Reflecting on where we have been and what we have done, as we considered yesterday, can sometimes lead us to despair, a state of mind touched on earlier (see 14 December). Rather than being encouraged by recalling how God has shaped our lives, we end up discouraged by being forced to confront our failures and disappointments. Somewhere along the line, we took a wrong turning, messed up the chance we had, missed the boat. We cannot even take a perverse kind of pleasure in catastrophe, because our lives never achieved enough momentum to create catastrophe. They just went pear-shaped, slowly enough that we didn't notice where things were headed until it was too late to make a difference.

Today, New Year's Eve, it takes a lot of effort to avoid thinking about what might or might not lie ahead. In the coming year, we will continue to grow older; the younger generation will continue to rise up and overtake us, seizing opportunities that we once considered ours for the taking; we will come to anniversaries that remind us only of what we have lost, or perhaps threw away and now regret. As midnight comes round, we may long to stop the clock, or at least rewind it to the point where we felt that life was salvageable. Our response to the fireworks and fizzing party mood of the evening can end up as gloomy as the words of the Teacher in our Bible reading.

We should, of course, be aware of the possibility that our state of mind is due to undiagnosed depressive illness. Thankfully, these days there is less stigma attached to acknowledging such conditions, although how acceptable it is in church circles is still debatable. At the same time, however, we should be aware that this mindset may share characteristics with the attitude forthrightly described by the Desert Fathers, the Christian mystics of fourth- and fifth-century Egypt, as the sin of 'akedia' or 'accidie'. In his book *Words of Spirituality*, Fr Enzo Bianchi, Prior of the Bose Community in Italy, describes accidie as 'a sort of asphyxiation or suffocation of the spirit that condemns those who suffer from it to unhappiness by causing them to reject what they have or the situation... in which they live, and to dream about another situation that is unattainable'.[11] It is not the unhappiness that is most problematic, but the individual's response to it—rejection of the immediate circumstances, followed by unrealisable fantasy about a better life.

If it is not appropriate to address our feelings with medication or some kind of therapy, what can we do when our life feels as if it has reached a dead end? Is there a viable way forward or do we have to resign ourselves to a soul-destroying job or miserable marriage, broken friendships or empty horizons, under a leaden cloud of fantasising which makes reality that bit more dreary when we come back to ourselves? One solution, touted by some pop psychology, is to rescue ourselves, jettisoning what we consider to be unhelpful relationships or situations that hold us back from being all we deserve to be. In the process, however, we may end up changing the wrong thing yet again, fleeing difficulties that actually merit being worked through, unthinkable though that may seem at the moment. These days, there is a treacherous tendency to assume that if something is remotely difficult, it must be bad for us. That may well be the case—but by no means always.

The harder, far harder path involves changes that lack the drama of the dramatic walk-out, the cinematic packing of bags and striding away into the sunset to claim our rightful destiny. It involves being realistic about our present situation with all its limitations and frustrations, and the end of any kind of comfortably numbing denial. It involves taking responsibility for our lives as they are now, rather than escaping into wish-fulfilment daydreams or ascribing all our difficulties to wrongs done to us by others, whether spouses, parents, children, colleagues or church leaders. Whatever has gone wrong in the past, however badly we have been hurt (and we may realise the full extent of that hurt relatively late in life), we do not have to spend the rest of our days bearing a mental placard that proclaims us as victims, first and last.

Then, and most importantly, we can approach our heavenly Father and hold our situation, our selves, up to him in open hands. We don't have to pursue a macho agenda of 'seizing the day' but, rather, humbly offer everything that we are and everything that we have failed to be to God, asking him to heal and make whole what has been broken or stunted. Finally, we can trust that if we ask, we will receive; if we search, we will find (see Matthew 7:7–8). The consequences may not make for a dramatic testimony in the short term; it can be a long, slow road back to a life of purpose and meaning. If God is blessing us with a new year, though, he will also bless us with purpose and meaning, if we tell him that that is what we seek.

Our pilgrim party, too, is not doomed for ever to wander a maze of leylundii and tarmac. See—a sandwich delivery man approaches and he points us in the way that will take us back to the right road...

## For reflection

*'God is nowhere; God is now here.'* [12]

*

## 1 January
### (Naming and circumcision of Jesus)

# CHILDREN OF THE COVENANT

In Christ Jesus you are all children of God through faith, for all of you who were baptised into Christ have clothed yourselves with Christ. There is neither Jew nor Gentile, neither slave nor free, neither male nor female, for you are all one in Christ Jesus. If you belong to Christ, then you are Abraham's seed, and heirs according to the promise... God sent his Son, born of a woman, born under the law, to redeem those under the law, that we might receive adoption to sonship. Because you are his sons, God sent the Spirit of his Son into our hearts, the Spirit who calls out, '*Abba*, Father.' So you are no longer slaves, but God's children; and since you are his children, he has made you also heirs.

GALATIANS 3:26–29; 4:4B–7

After yesterday's cul-de-sac experience, we are now back on track and have finally passed beyond the city limits. Before Christmas we journeyed to a high place from where we could seek a wider perspective. Now we are headed in a direction that leads away from the hills and down to the sea. In case we forget the significance of today, we pass a succession of carnival floats, along with some rather cold and grumpy marching bands, gathering for a New Year's Day parade. Probably more than any other day in the calendar, this feels like the 'morning after the night before', but it is the last chance for some seasonal celebration before the long march of January brings (in the northern hemisphere, admittedly) short dark days, long dark nights and various unpleasant varieties of flu. It is also a chance, if we haven't done so already, to think up some resolutions to take into the new year.

Of course, in terms of the Church calendar, today doesn't mark a new beginning. The liturgical year runs from Advent to Advent, starting with the countdown to Christmas and then moving towards Lent, which takes us to Easter, followed by Ascension, Pentecost and the weeks of 'Ordinary Time' or 'Sundays after Trinity Sunday', bringing us back, eventually, to Advent Sunday. Along the way are a host of 'red letter days' (so called because they are traditionally printed in red in the Church calendar and eslsewhere) celebrating events in the life of Jesus, such as Epiphany, the Annunciation of his birth to Mary (nine months to the day before Christmas Day; it seems that the Son of God kept to his due date— other babies, take note!), and the Transfiguration, besides a number of other festivals including commemorations of the apostles and some saints. In the Church calendar, today is not New Year's Day but the festival of the Naming and Circumcision of Jesus.

We may ask why we should remember an event barely mentioned in the Gospels (only Luke records it, in 2:21). Retellings of the nativity story usually conclude with the family's settling in Nazareth after their return from exile in Egypt (Matthew 2:21–23), and then skip to Jesus getting left behind in Jerusalem, aged twelve, before moving on to the picturesque figure of John the Baptist. Luke is at pains to point out, however, that Joseph and Mary did 'everything required by the Law of the Lord' (2:39) for the birth of their firstborn. He was circumcised eight days later and, when 40 days had elapsed since the birth, his parents brought him to be presented in the temple, completing the purification rites for Mary and consecrating Jesus to the Lord God (see Luke 2:22–38). This event is commemorated in the Church calendar on 2 February as Candlemas. It is interesting to note, too, that, in keeping with the Law, Jesus was not given a name until circumcision. Until then, he was just Baby.

Jesus was a fully paid-up Jew, one of God's chosen people; he did not operate as a freelance agent, only coincidentally Jewish rather than, say, Roman (and, no, he wasn't a closet Englishman). As our Bible passage points out, he was not only 'born of a woman' but 'born under the law', and through the mystery of redemption he opened the way for everyone to become part of the family of Abraham: 'Abraham's seed… heirs according to the promise'.

In his letter to the believers in Galatia, part of modern-day Turkey, Paul argues that followers of Christ no longer need the physical sign of circumcision, because we are released from the constraints of the law to be children in God's covenant family—every one of us, whatever our origin (to paraphrase Galatians 3:28). Through his atoning death and resurrection, Jesus has opened the way for us all to become descendants of Abraham, thereby fulfilling the Lord's original promise to the patriarch that his offspring would be as countless as the stars (Genesis 15:5).

Far too many Christians remain ignorant of the Jewish roots of the faith; over my years as editor of *New Daylight* Bible reading notes, I have received a surprising volume of letters querying the number of readings from the Old Testament (OK, so it's a particular passion of mine—but, as I point out in my replies, it also constitutes the greater part of scripture. Besides, BRF does not stand for 'Bits-of-the-Bible Reading Fellowship'). Some readers comment that they have been told from the pulpit that the Old Testament is 'only for the Jews' and so merits only cursory attention from New Testament believers. To counteract this unhelpful assumption, there is a growing tendency to use the term 'Hebrew Bible' instead of 'Old Testament'. The former phrase reminds us that when Jesus spoke of 'the scriptures', he meant the Old Testament, not the Bible as we now have it. 'Old Testament' can have unhelpful overtones of 'superseded, outdated'— which it isn't; it's the start of the story. Not many people would read the final part of a trilogy and not bother with the earlier volumes.

Here's a New Year resolution: get hold of a good study Bible and read the New Testament letter to the Hebrews. Dick France's *People's Bible Commentary* volume on the letter is a very helpful accompaniment.[13] Like Paul's letter to the Romans, Hebrews sets out the scheme of salvation, but with a specific agenda of exploring how Christ is the embodiment and fulfilment of all that God longed to do through his chosen people: he is both great high priest and king, and the supreme sacrifice for sin. Indeed, we should not forget that the New Testament writers were steeped in the teaching and imagery of the Hebrew Bible, and would have expected their audience to be, as well. If we ignore the first two-thirds of scripture, we will not gain a full picture of the work and person of God and our understanding of our faith will fail to grow as it should. In addition, we will miss out on a whole lot of wonderful narratives, prophecy, wisdom and poetry.

## For reflection

*American pastor and writer John Ortberg has spoken of how the theme of sacrifice is woven through scripture like a scarlet thread. The Israelites in the wilderness were taught the pattern of atoning sacrifice for sin; God offers his own self in redeeming sacrifice for the sins of the world. We are his adoptive children and so we will surely find that sacrifice will in some way be part of our lives as Christians.*

✳

## 2 January

# FINDING SANCTUARY

The Lord is my light and my salvation—whom shall I fear? The Lord is the stronghold of my life—of whom shall I be afraid? ... One thing I ask from the Lord, this only do I seek: that I may dwell in the house of the Lord all the days of my life, to gaze on the beauty of the Lord and to seek him in his temple. For in the day of trouble he will keep me safe in his dwelling; he will hide me in the shelter of his tabernacle and set me high on a rock... Though my father and mother forsake me, the Lord will receive me... I remain confident of this: I will see the goodness of the Lord in the land of the living. Wait for the Lord; be strong and take heart and wait for the Lord.

PSALM 27:1, 4–5, 10, 13–14

In these final days of pilgrimage, our path is leading us through pleasant places. Under a sky blown clean blue by the fresh but not piercing wind, we are on a road that follows the contours of the land, rising and falling so that we begin to glimpse the sea ahead. Passing through a pretty village, we come to a sturdy little stone church, benches thoughtfully arranged in a sunny corner of the churchyard for the eating of pilgrims' packed lunches.

I have been intrigued to learn that the word *llan*, which prefixes so many Welsh place names, has the root meaning of 'enclosure', coming by extension to mean the local church (as in Llandudno—St Tudno's church; Llanbedr—St Peter's church, and so on). It signified a place to belong and be safe, the place where thanks were given for your birth, where your marriage was made in the sight of God and where, eventually, your body was laid to rest.[14] It reminds us, too, of the long tradition of the church offering sanctuary to those pursued by the law. Although that right was eventually abolished, in more recent times immigrants facing deportation have sometimes sought sanctuary in churches and cathedrals.

Creating 'safe space' means engendering an atmosphere where those present feel relaxed, able to speak candidly and express vulnerability without fear of criticism or ridicule. It is an approach common in therapeutic and other small group settings, where enabling mutual honesty is one of the primary goals. So often, hurt people survive the hurlyburly of life by hiding their true feelings behind various emotional masks, or they employ coping strategies ranging from the relatively harmless to the deeply unhelpful. It is only in 'safe space', a found sanctuary, that the masks can begin to be lowered, the strategies laid aside and the work of healing begun.

The classic children's TV series *Bagpuss* features a 'saggy old cloth cat, baggy, and a bit loose at the seams'. The cat presides over a magical shop run by a little girl, who brings to it lost and broken things—a single ballet shoe, a pincushion, a toy elephant minus its ears. Each item is cleaned and re-stored to usefulness (or a new use found for it) by the other toys in the shop, which, like Bagpuss, come to life for the duration of each episode. The enduring appeal of the series is rooted in the way that every story hinges on the idea of safe-keeping, of something being brought to a place where repair and restoration are assured, no matter how dirty or damaged its original state.

Our reading from Psalm 27 exudes an air of safety, security

and serenity. The psalmist knows that God can be trusted for sanctuary and protection, even in the most miserable of conditions. The Lord provides an unshakeable foundation, a shelter in the 'day of trouble', such that the psalmist can wait with confidence and hope for the revelation of the goodness of God, right here, right now. As we read these verses, we can pray for a similar measure of trust and faith, so that we too remember that God is our light and our salvation, no matter how difficult life may be at present. And, in trusting God as our salvation, we can be bold enough to ask for rescue, for him to find us a place of sanctuary.

At a particular time of brokenness and unhappiness, someone I know well decided to try attending a church of a radically different worship tradition from the one with which she was familiar. She went along with some trepidation, worrying that the congregation might be a bit superior, a bit intolerant of those who did not 'know the rules'—and what about her noisy toddler? As she stepped through the door, however, toddler clinging to her hand, she was greeted by an older man who smiled at them both and said, 'You are welcome here.' Those words, together with the smile, touched her heart, conveying a much-needed reminder of God's love and care. She became a member of that church until she moved away a few months later, and for as long as it was her spiritual home it continued to provide sanctuary, a place where she sensed God's presence drawing close to her.

While the universal Church is Christ's body on earth (Colossians 1:24), the local church is the most obvious community 'store front' for faith, where people may venture to see what this religion business is all about. Given the human propensity for squabbling, nitpicking and excluding those who don't fit in, we may despair at the thought of our own church ever being a place of welcome, let alone sanctuary. Even if we like our home fellowship, we may feel daunted by the mega-show down the road that offers a five-star welcome service and turbo-charged worship. We may ask ourselves why anybody would want to join us.

The good news is that God is not as fussy as we are about where and how he chooses to work. He doesn't prioritise one type of church over another; he looks for people who are attuned to his voice, who humbly offer themselves in his service. Churches can be large and dysfunctional—or small and dysfunctional. Equally, they can be infused with the Spirit of God, regardless of membership roll, location or churchmanship. Yesterday's reading reminded us that in becoming Christians, we become members of God's family—and the church is where the family gathers together, where the members are at home. Like any 'blended family', we are not all the same and our backgrounds may be very different, but we are held together in the Father's love. Nurtured in his care and in the security of his embrace, we begin to share a family likeness, a kinship transcending every other bond. Together we can build a home that offers not only sanctuary and a general sense of belonging, but, at the centre, a relationship that lasts for eternity.

## For reflection

*Here's another New Year resolution: think about your own church, perhaps in discussion with others. How do you think it appears to the local community. Is it a fortress, keeping the world at bay? Is it a temporary resting place for those on a journey? Is it a welcoming family home?*

*

## 3 January

# FINDING OUR STRENGTH

Do you not know? Have you not heard? The Lord is the
everlasting God, the Creator of the ends of the earth. He will
not grow tired or weary, and his understanding no one can
fathom. He gives strength to the weary and increases the power
of the weak. Even youths grow tired and weary, and young
men stumble and fall; but those who hope in the Lord will
renew their strength. They will soar on wings like eagles; they
will run and not grow weary, they will walk and not be faint.
ISAIAH 40:28–31

After so many days of pilgrimage, we should be a bit fitter
and leaner than when we started out, Christmas excesses
notwithstanding. As we stride along the road, under a sunlit
sky, we may well be feeling energetic, resourceful and ready
to take on all that the later weeks of January may bring us
in terms of either bad weather or sickness. If we decide to
embark on a fitness regime, perhaps coinciding with the new
year (when so many gym memberships are taken out, with
such high hopes), we may not realise how much stronger
we are growing until one day we run for a bus or try to lift
a heavy box and find, to our surprise, that we now possess
unexpected muscles and new reserves of stamina.

The image of the Christian believer as an athlete in
training was used more than once by Paul to speak of discipline, endurance and the heavenly prize in view at the

end of the race of life (see, for example, 2 Timothy 4:7–8; 1 Corinthians 9:24–27; Philippians 3:12–14). Coupled with his characteristically robust language ('I strike a blow to my body and make it my slave', for example), it can cause those disinclined to sporting effort to dismiss such imagery as representing 'muscular Christianity', a term that is sometimes used insultingly of any down-to-earth approach to faith and worship.

The idea that life as a Christian disciple involves hard work and self-sacrifice is, I think, likely to be overlooked in these days when a spirituality characterised by the 'come to me, all who are weary' approach is increasingly popular. In an effort to broaden its appeal, we can present Christian faith as little more than a short cut to psychological well-being, a universal panacea to the stresses of life today, with the advantage of being more affordable than psychotherapy. Out of sorts? Feeling too busy? Try a quiet day—think of it as no more demanding than a spa for the soul; read a book of blessed little thoughts—you won't find it taxing; come forward for prayer—you'll feel much better straight away, we promise.

In the rush to rediscover ancient church traditions, especially any with a Celtic tinge, there has been a notable lack of people advocating the discipline of penance and the tradition of asceticism, although both of these are suitably ancient and were considered a vital part of discipleship in previous eras. To quote Fr Enzo Bianchi again: 'The current cultural myth of spontaneity... which sees effort and authenticity as opposed to one another, is a serious obstacle to human maturation and makes it difficult for us to understand why asceticism is essential to spiritual growth.'[15]

Growing spiritually stronger takes effort on our part, not least the effort of turning to God and tuning in to his presence, but such effort brings untold benefits. While a good many Christians—whom we might characterise as the keep-fit enthusiasts—are pleased to rise to the challenge and love any talk of discipline, goals and exercises, there are others who instinctively slide down in their chairs/pews and lower their gaze when the teaching takes that kind of direction. Some are likely to constitute what could be described as a 'disaffected fringe', comfortably settled on the margins of congregational life, where they can tuck into the theological food, criticise when it isn't up to the usual standard, and generally receive rather than give in any meaningful way.

Others (to put it rather bluntly) could be characterised as spiritual hypochondriacs. They may well have once been in need of care and support, but they have settled into a role in which they are always the cared-for, never the carers. They are hyper-alert to any twinge of personal weakness and neediness, and are eager for whatever Christian therapy or top-up is currently on offer—and lots of it. It would not occur to them to think about how God has gifted them, because they cannot see beyond their status as 'walking wounded', no matter how much healing prayer and TLC is lavished upon them.

Here is a New Year challenge for both the disaffected and the perpetually needy: start to think about finding your strength in God. Whether we feel weak through inertia or because we cannot believe that our legs will actually hold our weight, God may be calling us to a spot of bodybuilding—or at least to taking the first tentative steps forward on our own, however shaky we may feel. If we are accustomed to receiving, perhaps the time has come for us to find opportunities to give. We may feel that we have nothing worthwhile to offer, but remember how, in yesterday's reading, it was no more than a smile and a few kind words that touched my friend's heart. They were the means of God's grace for her at that moment, rather than a polished sermon, powerful testimony or superbly choreographed Solemn Mass. As it happens, we may already have been a source of blessing to others without being aware of it. We cannot know the full significance of what we have already done and the lives we have already touched.

It may be, too, that part of finding our own strength involves moving on from a congregation where we fit a little too comfortably into roles that demand little of us. Rather than staying on the margins and being disaffected, maybe it is time for us to follow God's lead and go off to join a new church family (sharing our decision with our church leadership first), where we will find fresh opportunities for service and perhaps unfamiliar patterns of worship to startle us out of complacency and stretch our souls. Instead of being perpetually needy, we may discover that we have gifts to share, that what we consider our second-rate efforts are precisely what the struggling minister down the road longs for, to help shore up a work that is only just beginning.

Do we recognise ourselves as needy, as disaffected—or as quietly confident in our God-given strength? If we sense that strength within us, we should give thanks and renew the dedication of our energies to God. If we fear that we couldn't possibly face any kind of challenge, however, we should take heart from today's Bible passage. Going out in the strength of the Lord, we are plugged into an endlessly renewable energy supply, one that builds up and does not overwhelm the weak, so we need not fear that his power will be too great for us. God wants us to grow stronger, and he will provide all that we need for this growth to happen. The promise is

of strength and stamina surpassing even that of 'youths'—
and we should remember that those who bother to train for
a marathon, however elderly they are, will manage to reach
the finishing line while the ostensibly fitter and younger (but
unprepared) have faded away miles previously.

## Reflection

*'I run in the path of your commands, for you have set my heart free'*
(Psalm 119:32).

*

## 4 January

# KEEPING SAFE

Put on the full armour of God, so that you can take your stand against the devil's schemes. For our struggle is not against flesh and blood, but against the rulers, against the authorities, against the power of this dark world and against the spiritual forces of evil in the heavenly realms. Therefore put on the full armour of God, so that when the day of evil comes, you may be able to stand your ground, and after you have done everything, to stand. Stand firm then, with the belt of truth buckled round your waist, with the breastplate of righteousness in place, and with your feet fitted with the readiness that comes from the gospel of peace. In addition to all this, take up the shield of faith, with which you can extinguish all the flaming arrows of the evil one. Take the helmet of salvation and the sword of the Spirit, which is the word of God.

EPHESIANS 6:11–17

Our journey has very nearly come to an end now. We have left the little church behind, passed along the winding village street, and now, as we descend the final stretch of road to the coast, we see before us a wide bay, flanked by cliffs and bordered by an appealing expanse of sandy beach. Far out in the bay, we see a small rocky island topped by a white lighthouse. The tide is low at present, so the rocks are clearly visible, but when the sea rises again they will lurk treacherously below the surface. The lighthouse is not barring entry to the bay, but it is warning sailors to be vigilant, watchful of the conditions as they pass by.

Whether we are near the finish or at the start of our life pilgrimage as Christian believers, whether we are stepping out boldly in response to God's call or simply marking time, we will encounter some degree of spiritual opposition—the 'devil's schemes' cited in today's Bible passage as the threat against which we must be vigilant. As C.S. Lewis wrote in *The Screwtape Letters*, his celebrated novel of correspondence between a senior and junior devil battling for control of a man's soul: 'There are two equal and opposite errors into which our race can fall about the devils. One is to disbelieve in their existence. The other is to believe, and to feel an excessive and unhealthy interest in them.'[16]

Ignoring the possibility of such opposition means we may lower our defences against that which would pull us down, soil our friendships, discourage us and daunt us. On the other hand, too much focus on 'the dark side' can result in seeing demons lurking everywhere, and we may lapse into the error of dualism—the belief that the forces of evil and goodness, God and the devil, are matched against each other, battling for supremacy, with the final outcome uncertain. Such an attitude can leave us feeling too fearful ever to 'take our stand' in case we lose the fight, even though our reading from Ephesians assumes that all believers will be required to take such action.

Taking a stand means just that: readying ourselves to resist attack, maintaining our position rather than rushing out in a show of aggression and bravado. Sometimes the most powerful act of spiritual warfare is simply staying put in a difficult situation, refusing to give up and ignoring the tempter's insinuations about going back to the place that feels like home or finding a more congenial setting. There may indeed be strong forces of opposition, whether human or spiritual, ranged against us, but our Father may lovingly protect us from seeing the full extent of what we have to withstand. Our responsibility is not to worry about what might be the case, but to employ the protective weapons of faith at our disposal, thanks to the workings of the Holy Spirit. We heed the warning of the lighthouse about the hidden rocks—but our response is to take measures to keep ourselves safe, rather than being too scared to try to navigate past.

Tangible signs of our faith can prove effective and helpful in this context, while at the same time we keep in good repair our essential equipment of faith, truth, peace and so on. While we can save our garlic for the kitchen, we can embody our belief in God's protection by such acts as anointing with oil, receiving Holy Communion, praying in tongues, wearing or holding crosses, and also making the sign of the cross, especially if we are feeling under threat for some reason. We should always remember, though, that the enemy we face has already been comprehensively and eternally defeated through Christ's death and resurrection. As Paul writes, 'Having disarmed the powers and authorities, he made a public spectacle of them, triumphing over them by the cross' (Colossians 2:15). That is a fundamental truth which we must never allow ourselves to forget.

Although we sometimes experience episodes of powerful and blatant spiritual opposition, we will probably more often find ourselves under subtle forms of attack, as we considered on 29 December in relation to Jesus' temptations in the desert. If we are alert to it, we will detect a sly undermining, a creeping discouragement or nagging suggestion that drains our energy and enthusiasm for the things of God. Subtle attack is easier for the victim to overlook and therefore, perversely, more effective. Christians can easily get worked up over rebellious teenage behaviour ('Help! My son's turned into a Goth', for example—although I gather that, for the most part, Goths are soft-hearted people who write poetry and take particular trouble over their appearance); churches may collectively wring their hands over the popularity of Harry Potter, fearing that the youth group will decide for Dumbledore instead of Jesus. What can get overlooked as a result is the level of backbiting in a congregation, or the pastoral relationship edging into immorality, or the lack of proper leadership accountability, especially in the touchy area of expenses. Such overlooked issues can turn into the rocks that shipwreck us.

Here is a final suggestion for a New Year resolution: consider renewing your baptismal vows, an act that happens to be a traditional part of going on pilgrimage. The significance of baptism, whatever our age when we were originally sprinkled or dunked, is that it is a public sign that we have passed from darkness to light. We publicly reject the devil and all rebellion against God, repent of our sins and turn to Christ. In renewing those promises, we remind ourselves both of what we once declared (or what was declared on our behalf) and of the fact that we are signed and sealed as members of God's family, citizens of his heavenly kingdom. When we prepare our defences for the spiritual battle, we do so in his unconquerable and almighty strength.

## For prayer

*I arise to-day*
*Through a mighty strength, the invocation of the Trinity,*
*Through belief in the threeness,*
*Through confession of the oneness*
*Of the Creator of Creation.*

FROM *ST PATRICK'S BREASTPLATE*
(TRANSLATED BY KUNO MEYER, 1910, FROM THE OLD IRISH TEXT)

# The way ahead

Now, as we gather on the sandy beach, our pilgrimage reaches its conclusion. The air is perfectly still and the cloudless, pale sky appears to curve down at the horizon to meet the mirror-calm, pale sea. The countryside through which we have walked, and the city where we have sojourned, are restored to a rightful proportion, diminished by comparison with all that blue infinity. I spent my childhood on a small island (small compared with Britain, anyway) and for years afterwards I missed the experience of turning the corner of a street and seeing the sea spread out beyond, glittering with light. Such a vista exuded the possibility not only of a blissful day of playing but of the general largeness of life that lay ahead.

The shore is a good place to conclude our time together, to say our goodbyes and go our separate ways home. We may feel relieved ('At last that's over for another year!') or anti-climactic ('Hmm—could have been a bit better') or worried that getting back into the pre-holiday routine will mean that any change or progress in our faith will be lost in the general sense of 'same old life' that may have dogged us previously.

Even if our lives feel circular, though, we should not forget that time is linear; we always go forward, rather than being doomed to return to the beginning again and again. The story of salvation in which we live is linear, too: Christ died once, for all (see 1 Peter 3:18); one day he will come again to judge the living and the dead, as the creeds of the Church remind us. We are called to look forward to all that God will do with us and through us in the days to come. And we have a hope to sustain us, as Paul writes, 'that he who began a good work in you will carry it on to completion until the day of Christ Jesus' (Philippians 1:6). It is his work in us, not our desperate striving to keep him interested, which is the truth underlying everything.

*

## 5 January

# THE FOLLY OF GOD

For the message of the cross is foolishness to those who are perishing, but to us who are being saved it is the power of God... Has not God made foolish the wisdom of the world? For since in the wisdom of God the world through its wisdom did not know him, God was pleased through the foolishness of what was preached to save those who believe. Jews demand signs and Greeks look for wisdom, but we preach Christ crucified: a stumbling-block to Jews and foolishness to Gentiles but to those whom God has called, both Jews and Greeks, Christ the power of God and the wisdom of God. For the foolishness of God is wiser than human wisdom, and the weakness of God is stronger than human strength.

1 CORINTHIANS 1:18–25 (ABRIDGED)

As we move from the season of Christmas to the season of Epiphany in the Church calendar, it is thought-provoking to realise that (depending on when Easter falls in the year) it may not be too many weeks before we start to anticipate Ash Wednesday and the beginning of Lent. Some extra-keen pilgrims may be already planning a Lenten journey, perhaps with added penitential discipline; others will be deploring the unbelievably early arrival of chocolate eggs in the shops.

It is not inappropriate to begin to look ahead towards Lent, Holy Week and Easter, however, because without Jesus' death and resurrection, the events of Christmas would be meaningless. We would simply be left with some kind of Yule feast, enjoyable but with no contemporary spiritual significance; nobody would bother commemorating the birth of a first-century Jewish baby who grew up to be a skilled carpenter, married, had children and died at a great age in his obscure village in Palestine.

As our Bible reading spells out in stark terms, God's plan for salvation through Jesus would be judged as 'foolishness' by any worldly standard. Think about it: if you were formulating a strategy to save the human race and had the resources of eternity at your disposal, would you really choose God's way as revealed in scripture? Would that narrative make a plausible *Dr Who* script? The timeframe of events is too long, for a start, and the risks extraordinary, surely unjustifiable, given the human track record (including the track record of God's chosen people) of responding to divine overtures of relationship and offers of salvation. We are so familiar with the story, we forget that at every point those involved could have chosen differently: Joseph could have divorced Mary, John the Baptist could have followed the example of Jonah and run away from his prophetic ministry, Jesus could have despaired utterly in Gethsemane and asked his Father to release him from the fate awaiting him. The 'what ifs' are, frankly, hair-raising.

Today's Bible reading reminds us that even God's apparent foolishness is superior to our mortal wisdom. In comparison with him, all our human efforts, all our attempts at understanding, are laughable. As Paul tells it, there is a universal tendency to have fixed expectations as to how God will work: 'Jews demand signs and Greeks look for wisdom, but we preach Christ crucified'. The gospel message is 'a stumbling-block to Jews and foolishness to Gentiles but to those whom God has called, both Jews and Greeks, Christ the power of God and the wisdom of God'. In order to grasp it, we need the Father's perspective, rather than simply trying to make sense of it from our own point of view.

This is not to say, of course, that we abandon attempts to reason out our faith; what it does mean is that sometimes we have to follow the example of the shepherds after the visit of the angels on the very first Christmas night. They heard the message, accepted it and followed the instructions—and as a result they found their way straight to the manger. Contrast the supposedly 'wise men', whose story we will consider tomorrow, who concluded that a baby king must be born in a palace, and were thereby nearly the means of bringing Jesus' life to an extremely untimely end.

We tend to assume that we know best, cherishing our preconceptions rather than bringing them into the presence of God, prayerfully waiting and listening for him to guide us through his Spirit. This may be the case particularly if we are accustomed to announcing confidently, 'This is what the Lord wants us to do.' In consequence, when we are confronted with an approach or message that discomfits us, we may be inclined to dismiss it, but instead we should remember— as Paul wrote to the Christians in Corinth—'The person without the Spirit does not accept the things that come from the Spirit of God but considers them foolishness, and cannot understand them because they are discerned only through the Spirit... But we have the mind of Christ' (1 Corinthians 2:14, 16). Having the mind of Christ means that our heart and head, our feeling and thinking, begin to be transformed into the likeness of Christ.

That this has to be the work of God's Spirit, rather than our own efforts, is underlined by our tendency to make God in our own image, viewing him through the distorting lens of whatever culture is most familiar to us. If we have been brought up with certain norms of politeness, self-deprecation and emotional restraint, for example, we are likely to assume that God will be an idealised version of these norms, a kind of super-vicar. If we are a go-getting executive, we may envision him as definitely white-collar (not to say designer-suited), master of the boardroom, whose precious time we must be careful not to waste. What if God is not like that, though? What if he turns out to be ebullient, enthusiastic and constantly laughing at his own jokes, for example? What if, when we finally enter his presence, we discover that we spend much of eternity listening to all that he has longed to tell us? The runaway success of William P. Young's book *The Shack* is partly due to the imaginative—and provocative—depiction of the Trinity, including God the Black Mother. Whatever we may speculate, we can be sure of one thing: we have not imagined the half of him and of what he plans to do.

We will think more tomorrow about our responsibility to share the story of salvation in all its glorious foolishness; the challenge for today is whether we are open to the new work that God will be doing in our lives and in our church in the year to come, a work that we may be tempted to ignore or misunderstand if it doesn't fit our expectations. Perhaps we, like the apostle Peter, will hear the voice of Jesus asking us to trust him, metaphorically step out of the boat and walk on water (Matthew 14:25–33). Will we listen, or will we close our ears because we are not 'that sort of Christian'?

## For reflection

*'Forget the former things; do not dwell on the past. See, I am doing a new thing! Now it springs up; do you not perceive it?' (Isaiah 43:18–19).*

*

## 6 January (Epiphany)

# HOMEWARD BOUND

After Jesus was born... Magi from the east came to Jerusalem and asked, 'Where is the one who has been born king of the Jews? We saw his star when it rose and have come to worship him.' ... Then Herod called the Magi secretly and found out from them the exact time the star had appeared. He sent them to Bethlehem and said, 'Go and make a careful search for the child. As soon as you find him, report to me, so that I too may go and worship him.' After they had heard the king, they went on their way, and the star they had seen when it rose went ahead of them until it stopped over the place where the child was... On coming to the house, they saw the child with his mother Mary, and they bowed down and worshipped him. Then they opened their treasures and presented him with gifts of gold, frankincense and myrrh. And having been warned in a dream not to go back to Herod, they returned to their country by another route.

MATTHEW 2:1–2, 7–12 (ABRIDGED)

The 'Magi' or 'wise men', who appear only in Matthew's Gospel, represent 'the wealth and wisdom of the Gentile world, the deep yearning and generous worship of the nations beyond Israel, coming to greet God's royal Messiah' (as John Proctor tells us in his commentary on Matthew), while the guiding star signifies that creation itself is moved to acknowledge the wonder that has occurred. The apostle shaped his narrative so that the story would have deliberate resonance with Old Testament texts such as Psalm 72 and Isaiah 60—and John Proctor points out that even if some readers find the whole episode a bit incredible, they should not overlook the underlying thrust of the Gospel account: 'that the coming of Jesus is important enough for nations and creation to honour him, for tyrant thrones to tremble, and for all the glories of scripture to be recalled'.[17]

Even at the outset of the Gospel narrative, we have a sobering reminder of how earthly powers and authorities will react to the coming of God's Son into the world. Some will bow down and worship, bringing the costliest offerings they can afford. Others will accurately perceive a threat to the status quo and to their own carefully orchestrated systems of control—and their response will be fear, anger and even murderous rage.

When their visit was done, the wise men experienced further divine intervention via a dream to ensure that they did not reveal Jesus' whereabouts to Herod. Then they returned home with the news of what they had experienced. For us, reading the story in the light of everything that happened thereafter, we are reminded of how Jesus still draws us to himself, beginning to work in our hearts while we may yet know little or nothing of faith, and eventually sending us out again as bearers of his good news. I always find it rather reassuring to read in Matthew's account of the first sending out, at the time of Jesus' ascension, that 'some doubted' (28:17). Despite everything that had happened since Good Friday, despite having the risen Jesus standing in front of them, there were still some who remained unsure. For us, as for the doubters, there is the gift of the Spirit, who came at Pentecost to confirm God's presence with his people for ever.

Jesus told his friends that they would share his message 'in Jerusalem, and in all Judea and Samaria, and to the ends of the earth' (Acts 1:8); thanks to the Roman transport network, the message was able to spread unbelievably fast. Legionaries came in force to Britain in AD43, just ten years or so after the death of Jesus, and there may well have been Christians among them, bearing the seed of the gospel ready to plant in new soil. While 'unreached people groups' are still to be found in the more remote corners of the globe, Christianity has continued to spread and flourish, with more recently established churches (in sub-Saharan Africa, for example) now sending leaders back to minister in countries that sent out missionaries to them centuries ago.

Although the traditional model of mission overseas has close parallels with the old Celtic monastic idea of 'white martyrdom' (leaving home for ever for the sake of the gospel, as opposed to 'red martyrdom' or dying for your faith), we should reflect on the fact that the Magi returned to their own country, albeit by a different route. To those of a romantic and adventurous mindset, the call to spread the word in a far-flung location may be heard far more readily than the call to be a witness in the less exotic setting of their native country. That is likely to be the place where our testimony will have a more enduring impact, however. It will be hard work, certainly, and the backdrop may be less photogenic, the cuisine less adventurous for our palate, but it may just be where God would have us serve him, all things considered.

The Norfolk story of the legendary pedlar of Swaffham tells how one John Chapman, pedlar, dreamt that he had to go to London Bridge and good would come of it. He arrived there, but found nothing except a man who laughed at his foolish quest and told of his own dream: that he was in a village called Swaffham, next to a pedlar's house, digging under a nearby oak tree, and found treasure there. Rushing home, John dug into the ground as indicated by the dream and found pots of gold, which not only made him a rich man but enabled him to pay for the rebuilding of the tumbledown village church. As it happens, there really was a 15th-century churchwarden of St Peter and St Paul, Swaffham, whose name was John Chapman and who was recorded as making generous gifts towards the enhancement of the building.

We will find God's riches in the place where he has made us to belong, even if we have to journey away for a time in order to realise this truth. He made us, he knows us, and he is gracious enough to want to use us in the building of his kingdom. Yes, we may find that we are being sent far away—but we should not use this possibility as an excuse for closing our ears to God's call, as it just may be that he is calling us to come back home and stay, growing deeper roots where we are most readily planted and witnessing to the gospel hope we have, not to strangers but to those who have known and loved us our entire lives.

Now, as our pilgrimage comes to an end, our group draws together one final time on the shore to share bread and wine in a final eucharistic meal of remembrance and thanksgiving. We marvel once again at the unbelievable gift of God's own self for the salvation of the world, the events of Christmas and Easter brought together in the transcendent plan of salvation. We remember, too, that one of the names for this special meal is 'Mass', from the concluding words of the Latin service '*missa est*': 'it is the going out, dismissal'. God calls us, equips us and sends us, and now it's time to go—but wherever we go, and however long it takes, he will be going with us, every step of the way.

## For prayer

*'Send us out in the power of your Spirit to live and work to your praise and glory. Amen'*

FROM THE POST-COMMUNION PRAYER, *COMMON WORSHIP* (ORDER ONE)

*

# USING THIS BOOK
# WITH A GROUP

Although the 'daily readings' style of this book means that it is best suited for individual use, it can also be used as the basis for a series of group sessions. Obviously, this will work best if the group members have all read the material for a given week! See below for six sets of four questions based on the themes for each week, which aim to stimulate further thought and discussion, plus suggestions for a concluding time of prayer. Another approach would be simply to gather together and discuss which of the week's readings the group found most interesting or challenging.

1–7 DECEMBER: EAT, DRINK AND BE MERRY

1.  What's the best Christmas present you've ever received—and why?
2.  How can Christians get right the balance between festive celebration and a focus on the spiritual heart of Christmas?
3.  To what extent is 'good humoured' an accurate description of your church? How might it be possible to promote more—or less—laughter in your times together?
4.  What place do you feel silence should play in corporate worship and private prayer?

**For prayer**

Ask people to share their feelings about the coming Christmas celebrations and then bring them honestly before God.

## 8–14 DECEMBER: EARN ALL YOU CAN, SAVE ALL YOU CAN, GIVE ALL YOU CAN

1. What is your response to the overall heading for this week: 'Earn all you can, save all you can, give all you can'?
2. What might be described as the 'well-worn groove of expectation' in the worshipping life of your church? In what ways might it be appropriate to change or refresh it?
3. With whom do you empathise more in the story of the prodigal son—the older or the younger son—and why?
4. To what extent have you ever experienced a time of exile in your life?

**For prayer**

Pray that, this Christmas, God will deepen in you an understanding of the size—and scandal—of his grace and generosity, and what the implications might be for you as individuals as well as for your church.

## 15–21 DECEMBER: HEAVENLY PERSPECTIVES

1. How does your faith affect your views on environmental issues?
2. What single word would you use to describe God—and why?

3. Can you give an example from your own life, or the life of your church, of God's call to go 'off-road' in some way?

4. When sharing our faith with others, how do we find an appropriate balance between discussing human sinfulness and stressing God's loving invitation to relationship?

**For prayer**

Spend some time reflecting on the majesty and greatness of God, perhaps reading a psalm aloud together, and then giving thanks for his coming as Immanuel.

## 22–28 DECEMBER: PILGRIMS TO THE MANGER

1. Do you think children's nativity plays help or hinder their understanding of the full meaning of Christmas?

2. Which bit of the Christmas story do you find it hardest to believe—and why?

3. What practical steps can members of your church take to involve those who might otherwise feel excluded from the celebrations at this time of year?

4. In your opinion, how important are the post-Christmas saints' days? How might you try to be mindful of them?

**For prayer**

Bring before God all those for whom the Christmas holiday season is a hard time, for whatever reason, and ask him to surround them with his love and grant them his peace.

## 29 DECEMBER–4 JANUARY: TRAVELLING INTO TOMORROW

1. In general, do you tend to look for short cuts or do you prefer the scenic route? Discuss the advantages and disadvantages of your preferences.
2. To what extent do you feel that your church is a family? Is it a healthy and happy family or are there some areas that need some sorting out?
3. How important is the Old Testament in your understanding of the Bible? Which bits do you know better—and which bits remain a 'closed book'?
4. What do you consider to be a helpful understanding of spiritual warfare?

**For prayer**
Ask God to show group members which aspects of their lives particularly need his challenge or healing at this time; wait in prayerful silence for his response.

## 5–6 JANUARY: THE WAY AHEAD

1. Are you relieved that Christmas is over for another year or is it a season that you leave behind with regret? Why?
2. How significant do you find receiving Holy Communion? How important is it in the life of your church?
3. Thinking of the story of the pedlar of Swaffham, what or where might be the 'hidden treasure' in your own circumstances?
4. What has been the most helpful insight that you gained from these times of group discussion?

**For prayer**

Give thanks together for what you have learned over the past weeks and ask for God's blessing on the year ahead, naming specific issues relevant to group members as appropriate.

*

# NOTES

1. R.S. Thomas, 'Wrong?' from *Collected Later Poems 1988–2000* (Bloodaxe Books, 2004).
2. Charles Dickens, *A Christmas Carol* (1843; 1946 King Penguin edition, p. 69).
3. Sarah Maitland, *A Book of Silence* (Granta, 2008, p. 220).
4. See Annie Dillard, *Teaching a Stone to Talk* (HarperPerennial, revised edn 1988).
5. Bob Mayo, *Divorce—a Challenge to the Church* (BRF, 2008, p. 22).
6. Robert Macfarlane, *The Wild Places* (Granta, 2007, p. 157).
7. Kevin Scully, *Five Impossible Things to Believe Before Christmas* (BRF, 2009, p. 62).
8. Loveday Alexander, *PBC: Acts* (BRF, 2006, pp. 64, 65).
9. Andrew Jones, *Every Pilgrim's Guide to Celtic Britain and Ireland* (Canterbury Press, 2002, p. 8).
10. You can read more about Marie Ozanne and the German Occupation of the Channel Islands in Madeleine Bunting, *A Model Occupation* (Pimlico, 2004).
11. Enzo Bianchi, *Words of Spirituality* (SPCK, 2002, p. 18).
12. See Douglas Coupland, *Hey Nostradamus!* (HarperPerennial, new edn 2004).
13. Dick France, *PBC: Timothy, Titus and Hebrews* (BRF, 2001).
14. I learnt about the meaning of *llan*—plus much more—from the DVD *A Celtic Pilgrimage to Bardsey*, presented by Andrew Jones. This is available from Bangor Cathedral Bookshop, Cathedral Close, Bangor, Gwynedd LL57 1LH (£12.50 plus postage).
15. Bianchi, *Words of Spirituality*, p. 4.
16. C.S. Lewis, *The Screwtape Letters* (1941; 1999 HarperCollins Selected Books, p. 733).
17. John Proctor, *PBC: Matthew* (BRF, 2001, pp. 26, 27).